ntacting the Editors
ery effort has been made to provide accurate information in this publication, but changes
e inevitable. The publisher cannot be responsible for any resulting loss, inconvenience or
ury. We would appreciate it if readers would call our attention to any errors or outdated
ormation. We also welcome your suggestions; if you come across a relevant expression
t in our phrase book, please contact us: Berlitz Publishing, 193 Morris Avenue,
ringfield, NJ 07081, USA. E-mail: comments@berlitzbooks.com

irst Printing: August 2007
rinted in Singapore

Publishing Director: Sheryl Olinsky Borg
Senior Editor/Project Manager: Lorraine Sova
Editors: Antje Schaaf, Julia Krumme
Translation: Publication Services, Inc., Kathi Stock
Cover Design: Claudia Petrilli
Interior Design: Derrick Lim, Juergen Bartz
Production Manager: Elizabeth Gaynor
Cover Photo: © QT Luong/terragalleria.com
Interior Photos: p. 12, © Studio Fourteen/Brand X Pictures/AgeFotostock; p. 16, © Comstock
Images/Alamy; p. 17, © European Central Bank; p. 28, © allOver Photography/Alamy; p. 35.
© Roman Krochuk, 2006/Shutterstock, Inc.; p. 39, © graficart.net/Alamy; p. 51, © Ryan
McVay/Photodisc/Age Fotostock; p. 54, © INSADCO Photography/Alamy; p. 58, © Creativ
Studio Heinem/westend61/AgeFotostock; p. 60, © Paul Mayall/photolibrary.de; p. 74, ©
Fred Lyons/Cole Group/Photodisc Green/Getty Images; p. 83, © fStop/Fotosearch.com; p. 84,
© Photodisc/Fotosearch.com; p. 96, © PIXFOLIO/Alamy; p. 98, © Christoph & Friends/Das
Fotoarchiv/Alamy; p. 104, Ryan McVay/Photodisc/AgeFotostock; p. 106, Zefa RF/Alamy;
p. 110, © Dainis Derics 2007/Shutterstock, Inc.; p. 112, © Sean Nel, 2006/Shutterstock, Inc.;
p. 121, © Photodisc/Punchstock; p. 132, © Carsten Medom Madsen/Shutterstock, Inc.;
p. 136, © Medio Images/Fotosearch.com; p. 138, © Royalty-Free/Corbis; p. 141, © Photodisc
Fotosearch.com; p. 143, © Uli/Shutterstock, Inc.; p. 147, © United Pictures/Alamy;
p. 148, © Photodisc/Fotosearch.com; p. 150, © fStop/Alamy; p. 158, © graficart.net/Alamy;
p. 170, © Royalty-Free/Corbis

D0608731

I don't understand.	
Do you speak English?	ehn·gleesh
I don't speak German.	**Ich spreche kein Deutsch.** eekh shpreh·khuh kien doych
Where's the restroom [toilet]?	**Wo ist die Toilette?** voh ihst dee toy·leh·tuh
Help!	**Hilfe!** hihl·fuh

German
Phrase Book
&
Dictionary

Berlitz Publishing
New York   Munich   Singapore

Contents

3

Food

People

Fun

Special Needs

Resources

Dictionary

Pronunciation

This section is designed to make you familiar with the sounds of German, using our simplified phonetic transcription. You'll find the pronunciation of the German letters explained below, together with their "imitated" equivalents. This system is used throughout the phrase book; simply read the pronunciation as if it were English, noting any special rules below.

The German alphabet is the same as English, with the addition of the letter **ß**. Some vowels appear with an **Umlaut**: **ä**, **ü** and **ö**. Of note, German recently underwent a spelling reform. The letter **ß** is now shown as **ss** after a short vowel, but is unchanged after a long vowel or diphthong. In print and dated material, you may still see the **ß**; e.g., formerly **Kuß**, now **Kuss**.

Stress has been indicated in the phonetic transcription: the underlined letters should be pronounced with more stress than others, e.g., **Adresse, ah-<u>drehs</u>-uh**.

Consonants

Letter	Approximate Pronunciation	Symbol	Example	Pronunciation
b	1. at the end of a word or between a vowel and a consonant, like p in up	p	**ab**	ahp
	2. elsewhere, as in English	b	**bis**	bihs
c	1. before e, i, ä and ö, like ts in hits	ts	**Celsius**	<u>tsehl</u>·see·oos
	2. elsewhere, like c in cat	k	**Café**	kah·<u>feh</u>

Letter	Approximate Pronunciation	Symbol	Example	Pronunciation
ch	1. like k in kit	k	**Wachs**	vahks
	2. after vowels, like ch in Scottish loch	kh	**doch**	dohkh
d	1. at the end of the word or before a consonant, like t in eat	t	**Rad**	raht
	2. elsewhere, like d in do	d	**danke**	dahn·kuh
g	1. at the end of a word, sounds like k	k	**fertig**	fehr·teek
	2. like g in go	g	**gehen**	geh·uhn
j	like y in yes	y	**ja**	yah
qu	like k + v	kv	**Quark**	kvahrk
r	pronounced in the back of the mouth	r	**warum**	vah·room
s	1. before or between vowels, like z in zoo	z	**sie**	zee
	2. before p and t, like sh in shut	sh	**Sport**	shpohrt
	3. elsewhere, like s in sit	s	**es ist**	ehs ihst
ß	like s in sit	s	**groß**	grohs
sch	like sh in shut	sh	**schnell**	shnehl
tsch	like ch in chip	ch	**deutsch**	doych
tz	like ts in hits	ts	**Platz**	plahts
v	1. like f in for	f	**vier**	feer
	2. in foreign words, like v in voice	v	**Vase**	vah·seh
w	like v in voice	v	**wie**	vee
z	like ts in hits	ts	**zeigen**	tsie·gehn

8

Letters f, h, k, l, m, n, p, t and x are pronounced as in English.

Vowels

Letter	Approximate Pronunciation	Symbol	Example	Pronunciation
a	like a in father	ah	**Tag**	tahk
ä	1. like e in let	eh	**Lärm**	lehrm
	2. like a in late	ay	**spät**	shpayt
e	1. like e in let	eh	**schnell**	shnehl
	2. at the end of a word, if the syllable is not stressed, like u in us	uh	**bitte**	<u>biht</u>·tuh
i	1. like i in hit, before a doubled consonant	ih	**billig**	<u>bih</u>·leek
	2. otherwise, like ee in meet	ee	**ihm**	eem
o	like o in home	oh	**voll**	fohl
ö	like er in fern	er	**schön**	shern
u	like oo in boot	oo	**Nuss**	noos
ü	like ew in new	ew	**über**	<u>ew</u>·behr
y	like ew in new	ew	**typisch**	<u>tew</u>·peesh

Combined Vowels

ai, ay, ei, ey	like ie in tie	ie	**nein**	nien
ao, au	like ow in now	ow	**auf**	owf
äu, eu, oy	like oy in boy oy	oy	**neu**	noy

How to Use This Book

These essential phrases can also be heard on the audio CD.

Sometimes you see two alternatives in italics, separated by a slash. Choose the one that's right for your situation.

Essential

When does the bank *open/close*?	**Wann *öffnet/schließt* die Bank?** vahn *erf*·nuht/ *shleest* dee bahnk
I'd like to change *dollars/pounds* into euros.	**Ich möchte *Dollar/Pfund* in Euro wechseln.** eekh *mehrkh*·tuh *doh*·lahr/*pfoont* ihn *oy*·roh *vehkh*·zuhln
I'd like to cash traveler's checks [cheques].	**Ich möchte Reiseschecks einlösen.** eekh *mehrkh*·tuh *rie*·zuh·shehks ien·*ler*·zuhn

You May See...

ZOLL	customs
ZOLLFREIE WAREN	duty-free goods
ZOLLPFLICHTIGE WAREN	goods to declare

Ticketing

When's...to Berlin?	**Wann geht ... nach Berlin?** vahn geht ... nahkh behr·*leen*
– the (first) bus	**– der (erste) Bus** dehr (*ehr*·stuh) boos
– the (next) flight	**– der (nächste) Flug** dehr (*nehks*·tuh) floog
– the (last) train	**– der (letzte) Zug** dehr (*lehts*·tuh) tsoog

Words you may see are shown in *You May See* boxes.

Any of the words or phrases preceded by dashes can be plugged into the sentence above.

German phrases appear in red.

Read the simplified pronunciation as if it were English. For more on pronunciation, see page 7.

Pick-up [Chat-up] Lines

Can I join you?	**Kann ich mitkommen?** kahn eekh <u>miht</u>·koh·muhn
You're very attractive.	**Sie sind sehr attraktiv.** zee zihnt zehr aht·rahk·<u>teef</u>
Let's go somewhere quieter.	**Lassen Sie uns an einen ruhigeren Ort gehen.** <u>lah</u>·suhn zee oons ahn <u>ie</u>·nuhn <u>roo</u>·ee·geh·ruhn ohrt <u>geh</u>·uhn

▶ For email and phone, see page 49.

The arrow indicates a cross reference where you'll find related phrases.

Information boxes contain relevant country, culture and language tips.

i When addressing anyone but a very close friend, it is polite to use a title: **Herr** (Mr.), **Frau** (Miss/Ms./Mrs.), or **Herr Dr.** (Dr.) and to speak to him or her using **Sie**, the formal form of "you", until you are asked to use the familiar **Du**.

You May Hear...

Kann er♂/sie♀ zurückrufen? khan ehr♂/zee♀ <u>tsoo</u>·rewkh·<u>roof</u>·uhn

Can he/she call you back?

Was ist Ihre Nummer? vahs ihst <u>eehr</u>·uh <u>noom</u>·ehr

What's your number?

Expressions you might hear are shown in *You May Hear* boxes.

When different gender forms apply, the masculine form is followed by ♂; feminine by ♀.

Color-coded side bars identify each section of the book.

11

▼ Survival

Arrival and Departure

Essential

I'm on vacation [holiday].	**Ich mache Urlaub.** eekh <u>mahkh</u>·uh <u>oor</u>·lowb
I'm on business.	**Ich bin auf Geschäftsreise.** eekh bihn owf guh·<u>shehfts</u>·rie·zuh
I'm going to…	**Ich reise nach …** eekh <u>rie</u>·zuh nahkh …
I'm staying at the…Hotel.	**Ich übernachte im Hotel …** eekh ew·buhr·<u>nahkh</u>·tuh ihm hoh·<u>tehl</u> …

You May Hear…

Ihren Reisepass, bitte. <u>eer</u>·uhn <u>rie</u>·zuh·pahs <u>biht</u>·tuh	Your passport, please.
Was ist der Grund Ihrer Reise? vahs ihst dehr groont <u>ihr</u>·uhr <u>rie</u>·zuh	What's the purpose of your visit?
Wo übernachten Sie? voh ew·behr·<u>nahkh</u>·tuhn zee	Where are you staying?
Wie lange bleiben Sie? vee <u>lahng</u>·uh <u>blie</u>·buhn zee	How long are you staying?
Mit wem reisen Sie? miht vehm <u>rie</u>·zuhn zee	Who are you travelling with?

Passport Control and Customs

I'm just passing through.	**Ich bin auf der Durchreise.** eekh been owf dehr <u>doorkh</u>·rie·zuh
I'd like to declare…	**Ich möchte … verzollen.** eekh <u>merkh</u>·tuh … fehr·<u>tsoh</u>·luhn
I have nothing to declare.	**Ich habe nichts zu verzollen.** eekh <u>hah</u>·buh neekhts tsoo fehr·<u>tsoh</u>·luhn

You May Hear...

Haben Sie etwas zu verzollen? hah·buhn
zee <u>eht</u>·vahs tsoo fehr·<u>tsoh</u>·luhn

Do you have
anything to declare?

Darauf müssen Sie Zoll zahlen.
dahr·<u>owf</u> <u>mew</u>·suhn zee tsol tsah·luhn

You must pay duty
on this.

Öffnen Sie diese Tasche. <u>erf</u>·nuhn zee
<u>dee</u>·zuh <u>tah</u>·shuh

Open this bag.

You May See...

ZOLL	customs
ZOLLFREIE WAREN	duty-free goods
ZOLLPFLICHTIGE WAREN	goods to declare
NICHTS ZU VERZOLLEN	nothing to declare
PASSKONTROLLE	passport control
POLIZEI	police

Money and Banking

Essential

Where's...?

Wo ist ...? voh ihst ...

– the ATM

– **der Bankautomat** dehr <u>bahnk</u>·ow·toh·maht

– the bank

– **die Bank** dee bahnk

– the currency
exchange

– **die Wechselstube** dee <u>vehkh</u>·zuhl·shtoo·buh

When does the
bank *open/close*?

Wann *öffnet/schließt* die Bank? vahn <u>erf</u>·nuht/
shleest dee bahnk

I'd like to change *dollars/pounds* into euros.

Ich möchte *Dollar/Pfund* in Euro wechseln. eekh <u>mehrkh</u>·tuh *<u>doh</u>·lahr/pfoont* ihn <u>oy</u>·roh <u>vehkh</u>·zuhln

I'd like to cash traveler's checks [cheques].

Ich möchte Reiseschecks einlösen. eekh <u>mehrkh</u>·tuh <u>rie</u>·zuh·shehks ien·<u>ler</u>·zuhn

ATM, Bank and Currency Exchange ———

I'd like to change money.

Ich möchte Geld wechseln. eekh <u>mehrkh</u>·tuh gehlt <u>vehkh</u>·zuhln

What's the exchange *rate/fee*?

Was ist *der Wechselkurs/die Gebühr*? vahs ihst *dehr <u>vehkh</u>·zuhl·koors/dee guh·<u>bewr</u>*

I think there's a mistake.

Ich glaube, hier stimmt etwas nicht. eekh <u>glow</u>·buh heer shtihmt <u>eht</u>·vahs neekht

I lost my traveler's checks [cheques].

Ich habe meine Reiseschecks verloren. eekh <u>hah</u>·buh <u>mie</u>·nuh <u>rie</u>·zuh·shecks fehr·<u>loh</u>·ruhn

My card *was stolen/doesn't work*.

Meine Karte *wurde gestohlen/funktioniert nicht*. <u>mie</u>·nuh <u>kahr</u>·tuh *<u>voor</u>·duh guh·<u>shtoh</u>·luhn/foonk·tzyoh·<u>neert</u>* neekht

My card was lost.

Ich habe meine Karte verloren. eek <u>hah</u>·buh <u>mie</u>·nuh <u>kahr</u>·tuh fehr·<u>loh</u>·ruhn

The ATM ate my card.

Der Bankautomat hat meine Karte eingezogen. dehr <u>bahnk</u>·ow·toh·maht haht <u>mie</u>·nuh <u>kahr</u>·tuh <u>ien</u>·geh·tsoh·ghun

▶For numbers, see page 167.

i The best rates for exchanging money will be found at banks. You can also change money at travel agencies, currency exchange offices and hotels, though the rate may not be as good. Traveler's checks are accepted at most banks (though banks are not required to accept them) and currency exchange offices, but a variable fee will be charged. Cash can be obtained from **Bankautomaten** (ATMs) with many international bank and credit cards. ATMs are multilingual, so English-language instructions can be selected. Remember to bring your passport when you want to change money.

You May See...

KARTE HIER EINFÜHREN	insert card here
ABBRECHEN	cancel
LÖSCHEN	clear
EINGEBEN	enter
PIN-NUMMER	PIN
ABHEBUNG	withdrawal
VOM GIROKONTO	from checking [current account]
VOM SPARKONTO	from savings
QUITTUNG	receipt

You May See…

German currency is the **Euro €**, divided into 100 **Cent**.
Coins: 1, 2, 5, 10, 20, 50 **Cent**; €1, 2
Notes: €5, 10, 20, 50, 100, 200, 500

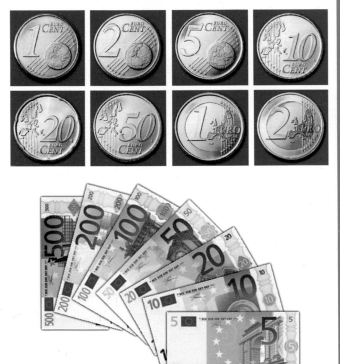

Transportation

Essential

How do I get to town?	**Wie komme ich in die Stadt?** vee <u>koh</u>·muh eekh ihn dee shtaht
Where's…?	**Wo ist …?** voh ihst …
– the airport	– **der Flughafen** dehr <u>flook</u>·hah·fuhn
– the train [railway] station	– **der Bahnhof** dehr <u>bahn</u>·hohf
– the bus station	– **die Bushaltestelle** dee <u>boos</u>·hahl·tuh·shteh·luh
– the subway [underground] station	– **die U-Bahn-Haltestelle** dee <u>oo</u>·bahn·<u>hahl</u>·tuh·shteh·luh
How far is it?	**Wie weit ist es?** vee viet ihst ehs
Where do I buy a ticket?	**Wo kann ich eine Fahrkarte kaufen?** voh kahn eekh <u>ie</u>·nuh <u>fahr</u>·kahr·tuh <u>kow</u>·fuhn
A *one-way/round-trip [return]* ticket to…	***Ein Einzelticket/Eine Fahrkarte für Hin- und Rückfahrt* nach …** ien ien·tsehl·tee·kuht/<u>ie</u>·nuh <u>fahr</u>·kahr·tuh fewr hihn oond <u>rewk</u>·fahrt nahkh …
How much?	**Wie viel kostet es?** vee feel <u>kohs</u>·tuht ehs
Which gate?	**Welches Gate?** <u>vehl</u>·khehs <u>geht</u>
Which line?	**Welche Linie?** <u>vehl</u>·khuh <u>leen</u>·yah
Which platform?	**Welcher Bahnsteig?** <u>vehl</u>·khehr <u>bahn</u>·shtieg
Where can I get a taxi?	**Wo finde ich ein Taxi?** voh <u>fihn</u>·duh eekh ien <u>tahk</u>·see
Take me to this address, please.	**Bitte fahren Sie mich zu dieser Adresse.** <u>biht</u>·tuh <u>fah</u>·ruhn zee meekh tsoo dee·zehr ah·<u>dreh</u>·suh
Can I have a map, please?	**Können Sie mir bitte einen Stadtplan geben?** <u>ker</u>·nuhn zee mihr <u>biht</u>·tuh <u>ien</u>·uhn <u>shtaht</u>·plahn <u>geh</u>·behn

Ticketing

When's…to Berlin?	**Wann geht … nach Berlin?** vahn geht … nahhk behr·leen
– the (first) bus	– **der (erste) Bus** dehr (ehr·stuh) boos
– the (next) flight	– **der (nächste) Flug** dehr (nehks·tuh) floog
– the (last) train	– **der (letzte) Zug** dehr (lehts·tuh) tsoog
Where do I buy…?	**Wo kaufe ich …?** voh kow·fuh eekh …
One/Two airline ticket(s), please.	***Ein/Zwei* Ticket(s), bitte.** ien/tsvie tee·kuht(s) biht·tuh
One/Two (bus/train/ subway) ticket(s), please.	***Ein/Zwei* Fahrkarte(n), bitte.** ien/tsvie fahr·kahr·tuh(n) biht·tuh
For *today/tomorrow*.	**Für *heute/morgen*.** fewr hoy·tuh/mohr·guhn

▶ For days, see page 170.

▶ For time, see page 169.

A…(airline) ticket.	**Ein … Ticket.** ien … tee·kuht
– one-way	– **einfaches** ien·fah·khuhs
– first class	– **Erste-Klasse-** ehr·stuh·klah·suh
– business class	– **Business-Class-** bihz·nehs·klahs
– economy class	– **Economy-Class-** eh·koh·noh·mee·klahs
– round-trip [return]	– **Hin- und Rückflug-** hihn oont rewk·floog
A…(bus/train/ subway) ticket.	**Eine …** ie·nuh …
– one-way	– **Einzelfahrkarte** ien·zuhl·fahr·karh·tuh
– round-trip [return]	– **Hin- und Rückfahrkarte** hihn oont rewk·fahr·kahr·tuh
– first class	– **Erste-Klasse-Fahrkarte** ehr·stuh·klah·suh·fahr·karh·tuh

How much?	**Wie viel kostet es?** vee feel <u>kohs</u>·tuht ehs
Is there a… discount?	**Gibt es eine Ermäßigung für …?** gihpt ehs ie·nuh ehr·<u>meh</u>·see·goong fewr …
– child	**– Kinder** <u>kihn</u>·dehr
– student	**– Studenten** shtoo·<u>dehn</u>·tuhn
– senior citizen	**– Rentner** <u>rehnt</u>·nehr
– tourist	**– Touristen** too·<u>rih</u>·stuhn
The *express/local bus/train*, please.	**Den *Express-/Nahverkehrs- Bus/Zug,* bitte.** dehn ehks·<u>prehs</u>·/<u>nah</u>·fuhr·<u>kehrs</u>·boos/ tsoog <u>biht</u>·tuh
I have *an airline/ a train* e-ticket.	**Ich habe ein *E-Ticket/Online-Ticket.*** eekh <u>hah</u>·buh ien <u>ay</u>·tee·keht/<u>ohn</u>·lien·<u>tee</u>·keht
Can I buy a ticket on the *bus/train*?	**Kann ich im *Bus/Zug* eine Fahrkarte kaufen?** kahn eekh ihm *boos/tsoog* <u>ie</u>·nuh <u>fahr</u>·kahr·tuh <u>kow</u>·fuhn
I'd like to… my reservation.	**Ich möchte meine Reservierung …** eekh <u>merkh</u>·tuh <u>mie</u>·nuh reh·zehr·<u>vee</u>·roong …
– cancel	**– stornieren** shtohr·<u>nee</u>·ruhn
– change	**– ändern** <u>ehn</u>·dehrn
– confirm	**– bestätigen** beh·<u>shtay</u>·tee·guhn

Plane

Getting to the Airport

How much is a taxi to the airport?	**Was kostet ein Taxi zum Flughafen?** vahs <u>kohs</u>·tuht ien <u>tahk</u>·see tsoom <u>flook</u>·hah·fuhn
To…Airport, please.	**Zum Flughafen …, bitte.** tsoom <u>flook</u>·hah·fuhn … <u>biht</u>·tuh
My airline is…	**Meine Fluggesellschaft ist …** <u>mie</u>·nuh <u>floo</u>·geh·zehl·shahft ihst …
My flight leaves at…	**Mein Flug geht um …** mien floog geht oom …

I'm in a rush.	**Ich habe es eilig.** eekh <u>hah</u>·buh ehs <u>ie</u>·leek
Can you take an alternate route?	**Können Sie eine andere Strecke fahren?** <u>ker</u>·nuhn zee <u>ie</u>·nuh <u>ahn</u>·deh·ruh <u>shtreh</u>·kuh <u>fah</u>·ruhn
Can you drive *faster/slower*?	**Können Sie *schneller/langsamer* fahren?** <u>ker</u>·nuhn zee *<u>shneh</u>·lehr/<u>lahng</u>·sah·mehr* <u>fah</u>·ruhn

You May Hear...

Mit welcher Fluggesellschaft fliegen Sie? meet <u>vehlkh</u>·ehr <u>floog</u>·geh·sehl·shahft <u>flee</u>·gehn zee	Which airline are you flying?
Inland oder international? <u>ihn</u>·lahnt <u>oh</u>·dehr ihn·tuhr·nah·syoh·<u>nahl</u>	Domestic or international?
Welcher Terminal? <u>vehlkh</u>·ehr tehr·mee·<u>nahl</u>	What terminal?

You May See...

ANKUNFT	arrivals
ABFLUG	departures
GEPÄCKAUSGABE	baggage claim
INLANDSFLÜGE	domestic flights
INTERNATIONALE FLÜGE	international flights
CHECK-IN	check-in
E-TICKET CHECK-IN	e-ticket check-in
ABFLUG-GATES	departure gates

Check-in and Boarding

| Where's check-in? | **Wo ist das Check-in?** voh ihst dahs <u>tshehk</u>·in |
| My name is... | **Mein Name ist ...** mien <u>nahm</u>·uh ihst ... |

I'm going to…	**Ich reise nach …** eekh riez·uh nahkh …
I have…	**Ich habe …** eekh hahb·uh …
– one suitcase	**– einen Koffer** ien·uhn kohf·fehr
– two suitcases	**– zwei Koffer** tsvie kohf·fehr
– one carry-on [piece of hand luggage]	**– ein Handgepäckstück** ien hahnd·guh·pehk·shtewk
How much luggage is allowed?	**Wie viel Gepäck ist erlaubt?** vee feel guh·pehk ihst ehr·lowbt
Is that pounds or kilos?	**Sind das Pfund oder Kilo?** zihnt dahs pfoont oh·duhr kee·loh
Which terminal?	**Welcher Terminal?** vehlkh·ehr tehr·mee·nahl
Which gate?	**Welches Gate?** vehlkh·uhs geht
I'd like *a window/ an aisle* seat.	**Ich möchte gern einen *Fensterplatz/ Platz am Gang*.** eekh merkht·uh gehrn ien·uhn *fehnst·ehr·plahts/plahts ahm gahng*
When do we *leave/arrive*?	**Wann ist *der Abflug/die Ankunft*?** vahn ihst dehr *ahp·floog/dee ahn·kuhnft*
Is the flight delayed?	**Hat der Flug Verspätung?** haht dehr floog fehr·shpeh·toong
How late?	**Wie viel?** vee feel

Das ist zu groß für Handgepäck. dahs ihst tsoo grohs fuehr <u>hahnd</u>·guh·pehk

That's too large for a carry-on [piece of hand luggage].

Haben Sie diese Taschen selbst gepackt? <u>hah</u>·buhn zee <u>dees</u>·uh <u>tahsh</u>·uhn sehlbst guh·<u>pahkt</u>

Did you pack these bags yourself?

Hat Ihnen jemand etwas mitgegeben? haht <u>eehn</u>·uhn <u>yeh</u>·mahnd <u>eht</u>·vahs <u>miht</u>·guh·geh·buhn

Did anyone give you anything to carry?

Leeren Sie Ihre Taschen. <u>lehr</u>·uhn zee <u>eehr</u>·uh <u>tahsh</u>·uhn

Empty your pockets.

Ziehen Sie Ihre Schuhe aus. <u>tsee</u>·uhn zee <u>eehr</u>·uh <u>shoo</u>·uh ows

Take off your shoes.

Wir beginnen jetzt mit dem Einsteigen ... weer beh·<u>gihn</u>·nuhn yehtst miht dehm <u>ayn</u>·shtayg·uhn ...

We are now boarding...

Luggage

Where *is/are...*?	**Wo *ist/sind ...*?** voh *ihst/zihnt ...*
– the luggage carts [trolleys]	– **die Gepäckwagen** dee guh·<u>pehk</u>·vah·guhn
– the luggage lockers	– **die Gepäckschließfächer** dee guh·<u>pehk</u>·shlees·fehkh·ehr
– the baggage claim	– **die Gepäckausgabe** dee guh·<u>pehk</u>·ows·gahb·uh
My luggage has been *lost/stolen.*	**Mein Gepäck ist *weg/wurde gestohlen*.** mien guh·<u>pehk</u> ihst *vehk/<u>voor</u>·duh guh·<u>shtohl</u>·uhn*
My suitcase is damaged.	**Mein Koffer wurde beschädigt.** mien <u>kohf</u>·fehr <u>voord</u>·uh buh·<u>shehd</u>·eekht

Finding Your Way

Where *is/are...*?	**Wo *ist/sind* ...?** voh *ihst/zihnt* ...
– the currency exchange	**– die Wechselstube** dee <u>vehkh</u>·zuhl·shtoo·buh
– the car rental [hire]	**– die Autovermietung** dee <u>ow</u>·toh·fehr·meet·oong
– the exit	**– der Ausgang** dehr <u>ows</u>·gahng
– the taxis	**– die Taxis** dee <u>tahks</u>·ees
Is there a...into to town?	**Gibt es ... in die Stadt?** gihbt ehs ... ihn dee shtadt
– bus	**– einen Bus** <u>ien</u>·uhn boos
– train	**– einen Zug** <u>ien</u>·uhn tsoog
– subway [underground]	**– eine U-Bahn** <u>ien</u>·uh <u>oo</u>·bahn

▶ For directions, see page 34.

Train

Where's the train [railway] station?	**Wo ist der Bahnhof?** voh ihst dehr <u>bahn</u>·hohf
How far is it?	**Wie weit ist es?** vee viet ihst ehs
Where *is/are...*?	**Wo *ist/sind* ...?** voh *ihst/zihnt* ...
– the ticket office	**– der Fahrkartenschalter** dehr <u>fahr</u>·kahrt·uhn·shahl·tehr
– the information desk	**– die Information** dee ihn·fohrm·ah·<u>syohn</u>
– the luggage lockers	**– die Gepäckschließfächer** dee guh·<u>pehk</u>·shlees·fehkh·ehr
– the platforms	**– die Bahnsteige** dee <u>bahn</u>·shtieg·uh

▶ For directions, see page 34.

▶ For ticketing, see page 19.

You May See...

BAHNSTEIGE	platforms
INFORMATION	information
RESERVIERUNGEN	reservations
WARTERAUM	waiting room
ANKUNFT	arrivals
ABFAHRT	departures

Questions

Can I have a schedule [timetable]?	**Kann ich einen Fahrplan haben?** kahn eehk <u>ien</u>·uhn <u>fahr</u>·plahn <u>hah</u>·buhn
How long is the trip?	**Wie lange dauert die Fahrt?** vee <u>lahng</u>·uh <u>dow</u>·ehrt dee fahrt
Is it a direct train?	**Ist das eine direkte Zugverbindung?** ihst dahs <u>ien</u>·uh dee·<u>rehkt</u> tsoog·ver·<u>bind</u>·ungh
Do I have to change trains?	**Muss ich umsteigen?** moos eekh <u>oom</u>·shtieg·uhn
Is the train on time?	**Ist der Zug pünktlich?** ihst dehr tsoog <u>pewnkt</u>·leekh

German trains are fast, comfortable and reliable. Train travel in Germany is a highly recommended alternative to driving. The **Deutsche Bahn AG** is the national railway of Germany. It offers many domestic and international routes. Tickets can be purchased at the station or through a travel agent. Buy your tickets in advance to get the cheapest fare and to guarantee seating. Many reduced-fare options are available; visit the **Deutsche Bahn AG** website or speak to a travel agent for more information.

Departures

Which track [platform] to…?	**Von welchem Bahnsteig fährt der Zug nach …?** fohn vehlkh·ehm bahn·shtieg fehrt dehr tsoog nahkh …
Is this the *track [platform]/train* to…?	**Ist das der *Bahnsteig/Zug* nach …?** ihst dahs dehr *bahn·shtieg/tsoog* nahkh …
Where is platform…?	**Wo ist Bahnsteig …?** voh ihst bahn·shtieg …
Where do I change for…?	**Wo steige ich um nach …?** voh shtieg·uh eekh oom nahkh …

Boarding

Is this seat available?	**Ist der Platz frei?** ihst dehr plahts frie
That's my seat.	**Das ist mein Platz.** dahs ihst mien plahts
Here's my reservation.	**Hier ist meine Reservierung.** heer ihst mien·uh reh·sehr·veer·roong
Can I open the window?	**Kann ich das Fenster öffnen?** kahn eekh dahs fehn·stehr erf·nuhn

You May Hear…

Bitte einsteigen! biht·tuh ien·shtieg·uhn	All aboard!
Die Fahrkarten, bitte. dee fahr·kahr·tuhn biht·tuh	Tickets, please.
Sie müssen in … umsteigen. zee mews·uhn ihn … oom·shtieg·uhn	You have to change at…
Nächster Halt … Hauptbahnhof. nehkh·stehr hahlt … howpt·bahn·hohf	Next stop…

Bus

Where's the bus station?	**Wo ist die Bushaltestelle?** voh ihst dee boos·hahlt·uh·shtehl·uh

How far is it?	**Wie weit ist es?** vee viet ihst ehs
How do I get to...?	**Wie komme ich nach ...?** vee <u>kohm</u>·uh eekh nahk ...
Is this the bus to...?	**Ist das der Bus nach ...?** ihst dahs dehr boos nahkh ...
Can you tell me when to get off?	**Können Sie mir sagen, wann ich aussteigen muss?** <u>kerhn</u>·uh zee meer <u>zahg</u>·uhn vahn eekh ows·<u>shtieg</u>·uhn moos
Do I have to change buses?	**Muss ich umsteigen?** moos eekh <u>oom</u>·shtieg·uhn
Stop here, please!	**Bitte halten Sie hier!** <u>biht</u>·tuh <u>hahlt</u>·uhn zee heer

▶ For ticketing, see page 19.

---

i

Bus and tram stops are marked by a green **H** for **Haltestelle** (stop). Larger cities, such as Berlin, Munich and Hamburg, offer 24-hour service. Service is limited on holidays and weekends.

In large German cities, the same ticket or pass can be used for the bus, subway, tram and above-ground train systems. Purchase tickets from the machines at bus stops or subway/tram stations. Check with a local travel agency or tourist information office about special discount tickets and offers.

You May See...

BUSHALTESTELLE	bus stop
STOPP-TASTE	request stop
EINGANG/AUSGANG	enter/exit
FAHRSCHEIN ENTWERTEN	validate your ticket

Subway [Underground]

Where's the subway [underground] station?	**Wo ist die U-Bahn-Haltestelle?** voh ihst dee <u>oo</u>·bahn·<u>halt</u>·uh·shtehl·uh
A map, please.	**Eine Übersichtskarte, bitte.** <u>ien</u>·nuh <u>ew</u>·behr·zehkhts·<u>kahr</u>·tuh <u>biht</u>·tuh
Which line for...?	**Welche Linie fährt nach ...?** <u>vehlkh</u>·uh <u>lihn</u>·ee·uh fehrt nahkh ...
Which direction?	**Welche Richtung?** <u>vehlkh</u>·uh <u>reekh</u>·toong
Do I have to transfer [change]?	**Muss ich umsteigen?** moos eekh oom·<u>shtieg</u>·uhn

28

Is this the subway [train] to…?	**Ist das die U-Bahn nach …?** ihst dahs dee <u>oo</u>•bahn nahkh …
How many stops to…?	**Wie viele Haltestellen sind es bis …?** vee <u>feel</u>•uh <u>halt</u>•uh•shtehl•uhn zihnt ehs bihs …
Where are we?	**Wo sind wir?** voh zihnt veer

▶ For ticketing, see page 19.

---

i

All main cities in Germany have an **U-Bahn** (underground subway), an **S-Bahn** (light rail system, above and below ground) or both. In most cities, the same ticket can be used for the **U-Bahn**, **S-Bahn** and bus and tram lines. Operating times vary for each city, but most operate from 4:00 a.m to midnight or 1:00 a.m. during the week, with some routes offering 24-hour service on weekends.

Most stations feature ticket machines; some may be in English.

You May See...

FAHRTZIEL	destination
EINZELFAHRT	one-trip ticket
TAGESKARTE	day pass
GRUPPENKARTE	group pass
WOCHENKARTE	weekly pass

Boat and Ferry

When is the ferry to…?	**Wann geht die Fähre nach …?** vahn geht dee <u>fehr</u>•uh nahkh …
Can I take my car?	**Kann ich mein Auto mitnehmen?** kahn eekh mien <u>ow</u>•toh <u>miht</u>•nehm•uhn

▶ For ticketing, see page 19.

You May See…

RETTUNGSBOOT	life boat
SCHWIMMWESTE	life jacket

i Ferry service across the Baltic Sea is available between Germany and Denmark, Sweden, Finland and Norway, or across the North Sea to the U.K. Ferry service is also available across Lake Constance to Austria and Switzerland. Boat trips are a fun way to explore the many rivers and lakes throughout Germany. Ferry and boat trips can be arranged by contacting your travel agent or searching the internet.

Bicycle and Motorcycle

I'd like to rent [hire]…	**Ich möchte gern … mieten.** eekh <u>merkh</u>·tuh gehrn … <u>meet</u>·uhn
– a bicycle	**– ein Fahrrad** ien <u>fahr</u>·raht
– a moped	**– ein Moped** ien <u>moh</u>·pehd
– a motorcycle	**– ein Motorrad** ien moh·<u>tohr</u>·raht
How much per *day/week*?	**Wie viel pro *Tag/Woche*?** vee feel proh *tahk/<u>vohkh</u>·uh*
Can I have a *helmet/lock*?	**Kann ich *einen Helm/ein Schloss* haben?** kahn eekh *<u>ien</u>·uhn hehlm/ien shlohs* <u>hah</u>·buhn

Taxi

Where can I get a taxi?	**Wo finde ich ein Taxi?** voh <u>fihnd</u>·uh eekh ien <u>tahk</u>·see
Do you have the number for a taxi?	**Haben Sie die Telefonnummer für ein Taxi?** <u>hah</u>·buhn zee dee tehl·uh·<u>fohn</u>·noom·ehr fewr ien <u>tahk</u>·see

I'd like a taxi *now/ for tomorrow at…*	**Ich brauche *jetzt/für morgen um …* ein Taxi.** eekh browkh·uh *yehtst/fewr mohrg·uhn oom …* ien tahk·see
Pick me up at…	**Holen Sie mich um … ab.** hohl·uhn zee meekh oom … ahp
I'm going…	**Ich möchte …** eekh merkh·tuh …
– to this address	**– zu dieser Adresse** tsoo deez·ehr ah·drehs·suh
– to the airport	**– zum Flughafen** tsoom floog·hah·fuhn
– to the train [railway] station	**– zum Bahnhof** tsoom bahn·hohf
I'm late.	**Ich bin spät dran.** eekh bihn shpayt drahn
Can you drive *faster/slower*?	**Können Sie *schneller/langsamer* fahren?** kern·nuhn zee *shnehl·ehr/lahng·sahm·ehr* fahr·uhn
Stop here.	**Halten Sie hier an.** hahl·tuhn zee heer ahn
Wait here.	**Warten Sie hier.** vahrt·uhn zee heer
How much?	**Wie viel kostet es?** vee feel kohs·tuht ehs
You said it would cost…	**Sie sagten, es würde … kosten.** zee zahg·tuhn ehs vewrd·uh … kohs·tuhn
Keep the change.	**Stimmt so.** shtihmt zoh

You May Hear…

Wohin? voh·hihn	Where to?
Wie ist die Adresse? wee ihst dee ah·drehs·uh	What's the address?
Es wird ein *Nachtzuschlag/ Flughafenzuschlag* berechnet. ehs veerd ien *nahkht·tsoo·shlahg/ floog·haht·uhn·tsoo·shlahg* buh·rehkh·nuht	There's a *nighttime/ airport* surcharge.

Car

Car Rental [Hire]

Where's the car rental [hire]?	**Wo ist die Autovermietung?** voh ihst dee <u>ow</u>·toh·fehr·miet·oong
I'd like…	**Ich möchte …** eekh merkh·tuh …
– a *cheap/small* car	– **ein *billiges/kleines* Auto** ien <u>bihl</u>·lee·guhs/<u>klien</u>·uhs ow·toh
– *an automatic/ a manual* car	– **ein Auto mit *Automatikschaltung/ Gangschaltung*** ien <u>ow</u>·toh miht ow·toh·mah·<u>teek</u>·shahl·toong/<u>gahng</u>·shahl·toong
– air conditioning	– **ein Auto mit Klimaanlage** ien <u>ow</u>·toh miht <u>klee</u>·mah·ahn·lah·guh
– a car seat	– **einen Kindersitz** <u>ien</u>·uhn <u>kihnd</u>·ehr·zihts
How much…?	**Wie viel kostet es …?** vee feel <u>kohs</u>·tuht ehs …
– per *day/week*	– **pro *Tag/Woche*** proh *tahk/<u>vohkh</u>·uh*
– per kilometer	– **pro Kilometer** proh kee·loh·<u>meh</u>·tehr
– for unlimited mileage	– **mit unbegrenzter Kilometerzahl** miht oon·buh·<u>grehnts</u>·tuhr kee·loh·<u>meh</u>·tehr·tsahl
– with insurance	– **mit Versicherung** miht fehr·<u>zeekh</u>·ehr·oong
Are there any discounts?	**Gibt es irgendwelche Ermäßigungen?** gihpt ehs <u>eer</u>·guhnd·vehlkh·uh ehr·<u>meh</u>·see·goong·uhn

You May Hear...

Haben Sie einen internationalen Führerschein? hah·buhn zee ien·uhn ihnt·ehr·nah·syoh·nahl·uhn fewhr·uhr·shien

Do you have an international driver's license?

Ihren Reisepass, bitte. eehr·uhn riez·uh·pahs biht·tuh

Your passport, please.

Möchten Sie eine Versicherung? merkht·uhn zee ien·uh fehr·seekh·ehr·roong

Do you want insurance?

Ich benötige eine Anzahlung. eekh buh·nert·ee·guh ien·uh ahn·tsah·luong

I'll need a deposit.

Bitte unterschreiben Sie hier. biht·tuh oont·ehr·shrieb·uhn zee heer

Sign here, please.

Gas [Petrol] Station

Where's the gas [petrol] station?

Wo ist die Tankstelle? voh ihst dee tahnk·shtehl·luh

Fill it up, please.

Bitte volltanken. biht·tuh fohl·tahnk·uhn

...euro, please.

... Euro, bitte. ... oy·roh biht·tuh

I'll pay *in cash/by credit card.*

Ich bezahle *bar/mit Kreditkarte.* eekh beht·sahl·uh *bahr/miht kreh·deet·kahr·tuh*

You May See...

BENZIN	gas [petrol]
BLEIFREI	unleaded
NORMAL	regular
SUPER	super
DIESEL	diesel

Asking Directions

Is this the way to…?	**Ist das der Weg nach …?** ihst dahs dehr vehg nahkh …
How far is it to…?	**Wie weit ist es bis …?** vee viet ihst ehs bihs …
Where's…?	**Wo ist …?** voh ihst …
–…Street	**– die … Straße** dee … shtrahs·suh
– this address	**– diese Adresse** deez·uh ah·drehs·uh
– the highway [motorway]	**– die Autobahn** dee·uh ow·toh·bahn
Can you show me on the map?	**Können Sie mir das auf der Karte zeigen?** kern·nuhn zee meer dahs owf dehr kahrt·uh tsieg·uhn
I'm lost.	**Ich habe mich verfahren.** eekh hahb·uh meekh fehr·fahr·uhn

You May Hear…

geradeaus geh·rahd·uh·ows	straight ahead
links leenks	left
rechts rehkhts	right
an der/um die Ecke ahn dehr/oom dee eh·kuh	on/around the corner
gegenüber geh·guhn·ew·behr	opposite
hinter hihnt·ehr	behind
neben nehb·uhn	next to
nach nahkh	after
nördlich/südlich nerd·leekh/zewd·leekh	north/south
östlich/westlich erst·leekh/vehst·leekh	east/west
an der Ampel ahn dehr ahmp·ehl	at the traffic light
an der Kreuzung ahn dehr kroytz·oong	at the intersection

34

You May See...

HÖCHSTGESCHWINDIGKEIT	maximum speed limit
ÜBERHOLVERBOT	no passing
VERBOT FÜR FAHRZEUGE ALLER ART	all vehicles prohibited
EINBAHNSTRASSE	one-way street
KEINE DURCHFAHRT	no entry
STOPP	stop
VORFAHRT GEWÄHREN	yield

Parking

Can I park here?	**Kann ich hier parken?** kahn eekh heer <u>pahrk</u>·uhn
Where's…?	**Wo ist …?** voh ihst …
– the parking garage	**– das Parkhaus** dahs <u>pahrk</u>·hows
– the parking lot [car park]	**– der Parkplatz** dehr <u>pahrk</u>·plahts
– the parking meter	**– die Parkuhr** dee <u>pahrk</u>·oor
How much…?	**Wie viel kostet es …?** vee feel <u>kohs</u>·tuht ehs …
– per hour	**– pro Stunde** proh <u>shtoond</u>·uh
– per day	**– pro Tag** proh tahk
– overnight	**– über Nacht** <u>ew</u>·behr nahkht

---

i

Parking on the street is common in Germany; look for 🅿 . You may see additional parking instructions located under the sign.

🅿 2 Std. Indicates that you can park there for the amount of time shown (in hours). Make sure your rental car company provides a parking disc when you pick up your car. Once parked, turn the dial to indicate the time you parked and put the disc on your dashboard where it is visible.

If you see mit Parkschein you must purchase a parking ticket from a nearby machine and place it on your dashboard where it is visible.

Parking lots and garages are other parking options. Most lots and garages use a self-pay system. When entering, obtain the time-stamped ticket from the machine. Use the machine near the pedestrian entrance to pay for parking; insert your ticket into the machine, pay the amount it displays and then remove the validated ticket. Proceed to your car and insert that ticket into the machine at the exit.

Breakdown and Repairs

Where's the garage?	**Wo ist die Autowerkstatt?** voh ihst dee ow·toh·<u>vehrk</u>·shtaht
My car *broke down/ won't start.*	**Mein Auto *ist kaputt/springt nicht an.*** mien <u>ow</u>·toh ihst <u>kah</u>·poot/shprihngt neekht ahn
Can you fix it (today)?	**Können Sie es (heute) reparieren?** <u>kern</u>·nuhn zee ehs (<u>hoy</u>·tuh) reh·pah·<u>reer</u>·uhn
When will it be ready?	**Wann wird es fertig sein?** vahn wirt ehs <u>fehr</u>·teekh zien
How much?	**Wie viel kostet es?** vee feel <u>kohs</u>·tuht ehs

Accidents

There was an accident.	**Es hat einen Unfall gegeben.** ehs haht <u>ien</u>·uhn <u>oon</u>·fahl guh·<u>geh</u>·buhn
Call *an ambulance/ the police.*	**Rufen *Sie einen Krankenwagen/die Polizei.*** <u>roof</u>·uhn zee <u>ien</u>·uhn <u>krahnk</u>·uhn·vahg·uhn/dee poh·lee·<u>tsie</u>

Accommodations

Essential

Can you recommend a hotel?	**Können Sie ein Hotel empfehlen?** <u>ker</u>·nuhn zee ien hoh·<u>tehl</u> ehm·<u>pfeh</u>·luhn
I have a reservation.	**Ich habe eine Reservierung.** eekh <u>hahb</u>·uh <u>ien</u>·uh rehz·ehr·<u>veer</u>·oong
My name is...	**Mein Name ist ...** mien <u>nahm</u>·uh ihst ...

Do you have a room…?	**Haben Sie ein Zimmer …?** <u>hah</u>·buhn zee ien <u>tsihm</u>·mehr …
– for *one person/ two people*	**– für *eine Person/zwei Personen*** fewr <u>*ien*</u>·uh pehr·<u>*sohn*</u>/tsvie pehr·<u>*sohn*</u>·uhn
– with a bathroom	**– mit Bad** miht bahd
– with air conditioning	**– mit Klimaanlage** miht <u>kleem</u>·uh·ahn·lahg·uh
For…	**Für …** fewr …
– tonight	**– heute Nacht** <u>hoy</u>·tuh nahkht
– two nights	**– zwei Nächte** tsvie <u>nehkht</u>·uh
– one week	**– eine Woche** <u>ien</u>·uh <u>vohkh</u>·uh
How much?	**Wie viel kostet es?** vee feel <u>kohs</u>·tuht ehs
Is there anything cheaper?	**Gibt es etwas Billigeres?** gihpt ehs <u>eht</u>·vahs <u>bihl</u>·lee·geh·ruhs
When's check-out?	**Wann ist der Check-out?** vahn ihst dehr <u>tshehk</u>·owt
Can I leave this in the safe?	**Kann ich das im Safe lassen?** kahn eekh dahs ihm sehf <u>lahs</u>·suhn
Can I leave my bags?	**Kann ich meine Taschen hierlassen?** kahn eekh <u>mien</u>·uh <u>tahsh</u>·uhn heer·lahs·suhn
Can I have *my bill/a receipt*?	**Kann ich *meine Rechnung/eine Quittung* haben?** kahn eekh <u>*mien*</u>·uh <u>*rehkh*</u>·noong/<u>*ien*</u>·uh <u>*kveet*</u>·oong hah·buhn
I'll pay *in cash/by credit card*.	**Ich bezahle *bar/mit Kreditkarte*.** eekh beht·<u>sahl</u>·uh *bahr/miht kreh·<u>deet</u>·kahr·tuh*

If you didn't reserve accommodations before your trip, visit the local **Touristeninformationsbüro** (tourist information office) for recommendations on places to stay.

Finding Lodging

Can you recommend…?	**Können Sie … empfehlen?** <u>kern</u>·uhn zee … ehm·<u>pfeh</u>·luhn
– a hotel	**– ein Hotel** ien hoh·<u>tehl</u>
– a hostel	**– eine Jugendherberge** <u>ien</u>·uh <u>yoog</u>·uhnd·hehr·behr·guh
– a campground	**– einen Campingplatz** <u>ien</u>·uhn <u>kahmp</u>·eeng·plahts
– a bed and breakfast	**– eine Pension** <u>ien</u>·uh pehn·<u>syohn</u>
What is near it?	**Was ist in der Nähe davon?** vahs ihst ihn dehr <u>neh</u>·uh dah·<u>fohn</u>
How do I get there?	**Wie komme ich dorthin?** vee <u>kohm</u>·uh eekh dohrt·<u>hihn</u>

i

Travelers have numerous accommodation options in Germany, from budget to luxury. A **Pension** (bed and breakfast) provides opportunities to experience life in a German home. **Jugendherbergen** (youth hostels) are also available, catering to travelers of all ages. **Urlaub auf dem Bauernhof** (farm stay) is a great way to see the countryside and enjoy rural Germany. In some areas, you may be able to find **Modernisierte Schlossunterkünfte**, old castles that have been converted into beautiful accommodations. **Ferienwohnungen** (vacation apartments) and **Ferienhäuser** (holiday homes) allow travelers to rent fully equipped apartments and villas throughout Germany. All options can be booked with travel agents, tour companies or on the internet.

At the Hotel

I have a reservation.	**Ich habe eine Reservierung.** eekh <u>hahb</u>·uh <u>ien</u>·uh rehz·<u>ehr</u>·veer·oong
My name is…	**Mein Name ist …** mien <u>nahm</u>·uh ihst …
Do you have a room…?	**Haben Sie ein Zimmer …?** <u>hah</u>·buhn zee ien <u>tsihm</u>·mehr …
– with a *bathroom [toilet]/shower*	– **mit** *Bad/Dusche* miht *bahd/<u>doo</u>·shuh*
– with air conditioning	– **mit Klimaanlage** miht <u>kleem</u>·uh·ahn·lah·guh
– that's *smoking/ non-smoking*	– **für** *Raucher/Nichtraucher* fewr *<u>rowkh</u>·ehr/ <u>neekht</u>·rowkh·ehr*
For…	**Für …** fewr …
– tonight	– **heute Nacht** <u>hoyt</u>·uh nahkht
– two nights	– **zwei Nächte** tsvie <u>nehkht</u>·uh
– a week	– **eine Woche** <u>ien</u>·uh <u>vohkh</u>·uh

▶For numbers, see page 167.

Do you have…?	**Haben Sie …?** hah·buhn zee …
– a computer	**– einen Computer** <u>ien</u>·uhn kohm·<u>pjoot</u>·ehr
– an elevator [a lift]	**– einen Fahrstuhl** <u>ien</u>·uhn <u>fahr</u>·shtoohl
– (wireless) internet service	**– (wireless) Internetanschluss** (<u>wier</u>·luhs) <u>ihnt</u>·ehr·neht·ahn·shloos
– room service	**– Zimmerservice** <u>tsihm</u>·mehr·sehr·vees
– a pool	**– einen Pool** <u>ien</u>·uhn pool
– a gym	**– einen Fitnessraum** <u>ien</u>·uhn <u>fiht</u>·nehs·rowm
I need…	**Ich brauche …** eekh <u>browkh</u>·uh …
– an extra bed	**– ein zusätzliches Bett** ien tsoo·<u>zehts</u>·leeks·uhs beht
– a cot	**– ein Kinderbett** ien <u>kihnd</u>·ehr·beht
– a crib	**– ein Gitterbett** ien <u>giht</u>·tehr·beht

You May Hear…

***Ihren Reisepass/Ihre Kreditkarte**, bitte.* <u>eehr</u>·uhn <u>riez</u>·uh·pahs/<u>eehr</u>·uh kreh·<u>deet</u>·kahrt·uh <u>biht</u>·tuh	Your *passport/credit card, please.*
Bitte füllen Sie dieses Formular aus. <u>biht</u>·tuh <u>fewl</u>·uhn zee <u>deez</u>·uhs fohr·moo·<u>lahr</u> ows	Fill out this form, please.
Bitte unterschreiben Sie hier. <u>biht</u>·tuh oon·tehr·<u>shrieb</u>·uhn zee heer	Sign here, please.

Price

How much per *night/week*?	**Wie viel kostet es pro *Nacht/Woche*?** vee feel <u>kohs</u>·tuht ehs proh *nahkht/<u>vohkh</u>·uh*

Does that include breakfast/sales tax [VAT]?	**Beinhaltet der Preis _ein Frühstück/ Mehrwertsteuer_?** beh·ien·hahlt·uht dehr pries ien _frewh·shtewkh/mehr·wehrt·shtoy·ehr_
Are there any discounts?	**Gibt es irgendwelche Ermäßigungen?** gihpt ehs eer·guhnd·vehlkh·uh ehr·meh·see·goong·uhns

Decisions

Can I see the room?	**Kann ich das Zimmer sehen?** kahn eekh dahs tsihm·mehr zeh·uhn
I'd like a…room.	**Ich möchte ein … Zimmer.** eekh merkh·tuh ien … tsihm·muhr
– better	– **besseres** behs·sehr·uhs
– bigger	– **größeres** grers·ehr·uhs
– cheaper	– **billiges** bihl·lee·gehr·uhs
– quieter	– **ruhigeres** roo·ee·gehr·uhs
I'll take it.	**Ich nehme es.** eekh nehm·uh ehs
No, I won't take it.	**Nein, ich nehme es nicht.** nien eekh nehm·uh ehs neekht

Questions

Where's…?	**Wo ist …?** voh ihhst …
– the bar	– **die Bar** dee bahr
– the bathroom [toilet]	– **die Toilette** dee toy·leht
– the elevator [lift]	– **der Fahrstuhl** dehr fahr·shtoohl
Can I have…?	**Kann ich … haben?** kahn eekh … hah·buhn
– a blanket	– **eine Decke** ien·uh dehk·uh
– an iron	– **ein Bügeleisen** ien bew·guh·liez·ehn
– the room key/the key card	– **den Zimmerschlüssel/die Schlüsselkarte** dehn tsihm·mehr·shlews·uhl/dee shlews·ehl·kahrt·uh

– a pillow	**– ein Kissen** ien <u>kihs</u>·suhn
– soap	**– Seife** <u>zief</u>·uh
– toilet paper	**– Toilettenpapier** toy·<u>leht</u>·tuhn·pah·peer
– a towel	**– ein Handtuch** ien <u>hahnt</u>·tookh
Do you have an adapter for this?	**Haben Sie hierfür einen Adapter?** <u>hah</u>·buhn zee heer·<u>fewr</u> ien·uhn ah·<u>dahp</u>·tehr
How do I turn on the lights?	**Wie schalte ich das Licht an?** vee <u>shahlt</u>·uh eekh dahs leekht ahn
Can you wake me at…?	**Können Sie mich um … wecken?** <u>kern</u>·nuhn zee meekh oom … <u>vehk</u>·uhn
Can I leave this in the safe?	**Kann ich das im Safe lassen?** kahn eekh dahs ihm sehf <u>lahs</u>·suhn
Can I have my things from the safe?	**Kann ich meine Sachen aus dem Safe haben?** kahn eekh <u>mien</u>·uh <u>zahkh</u>·uhn ows dehm sehf <u>hah</u>·buhn
Is there *mail [post]/ a message* for me?	**Haben Sie *Post/eine Nachricht* für mich?** <u>hah</u>·buhn zee *pohst/<u>ien</u>·uh <u>nahkh</u>·reekht* fewr meekh

You May See…

DRÜCKEN/ZIEHEN	push/pull
TOILETTE	bathroom [toilet]
DUSCHE	shower
FAHRSTUHL	elevator [lift]
TREPPE	stairs
WÄSCHEREI	laundry
BITTE NICHT STÖREN	do not disturb
FEUERSCHUTZTÜR	fire door
NOTAUSGANG	(emergency) exit
WECKRUF	wake-up call

Problems

There's a problem.	**Es gibt ein Problem.** ehs gihbt ien prohb-<u>lehm</u>
I lost my *key/my key card*.	**Ich habe *meinen Schlüssel/meine Schlüsselkarte* verloren.** eekh <u>hahb</u>-uh <u>mien</u>-uhn <u>shlews</u>-uhl/<u>mien</u>-uh <u>shlews</u>-ehl-kahrt-uh fehr-<u>lohr</u>-uhn
I'm locked out of the room.	**Ich habe mich ausgesperrt.** eekh <u>hahb</u>-uh meekh ows-guh-<u>shpehrt</u>
There's no *hot water/toilet paper*.	**Ich habe kein *heißes Wasser/ Toilettenpapier*.** eekh <u>hahb</u>-uh kien <u>hies</u>-suhs <u>vahs</u>-sehr/<u>toy</u>-leht-uhn-pah-peer
The room is dirty.	**Das Zimmer ist schmutzig.** dahs <u>tsihm</u>-mehr ihst <u>shmoot</u>-seek
There are bugs in the room.	**Im Zimmer sind Insekten.** ihm <u>tsihm</u>-mehr zihnt ihn-<u>sehkt</u>-uhn
The...doesn't work.	**... funktioniert nicht.** ... foonk-syoh-<u>neert</u> neekht
Can you fix...?	**Können Sie ... reparieren?** <u>kern</u>-nuhn zee ... reh-pah-<u>reer</u>-ruhn
– the air conditioning	– **die Klimaanlage** dee <u>kleem</u>-uh-ahn-lahg-uh
– the fan	– **den Ventilator** dehn vehn-tee-<u>laht</u>-ohr
– the heat [heating]	– **die Heizung** dee <u>hiets</u>-oong
– the light	– **das Licht** dahs leekht
– the TV	– **den Fernseher** dehn <u>fehrn</u>-seh-ehr
– the toilet	– **die Toilette** dee toy-<u>leht</u>-tuh
I'd like another room.	**Ich möchte gern ein anderes Zimmer.** eekh <u>merkh</u>-tuh gehrn ien <u>ahn</u>-dehr-uhs <u>tsihm</u>-mehr

---

i Voltage is 220, and plugs are two-pronged. You may need a converter and/or an adapter for your appliances.

Check-out

When's check-out? | **Wann ist der Check-out?** vahn ihst dehr <u>tshehk</u>·owt

Can I leave my bags here until...? | **Kann ich mein Gepäck bis ... hierlassen?** kahn eekh mien geh·<u>pehk</u> bihs ... <u>heer</u>·lahs·uhn

Can I have *an itemized bill/ a receipt*? | **Kann ich eine *aufgeschlüsselte Rechnung/ Quittung* haben?** kahn eekh <u>ien</u>·uh owf·guh·<u>shlews</u>·ehlt·uh <u>rekh</u>·noong/<u>kveet</u>·oong hah·buhn

I think there's a mistake. | **Ich glaube, hier stimmt etwas nicht.** eekh <u>glowb</u>·uh heer shtihmt <u>eht</u>·vahs neekht

I'll pay *in cash/by credit card*. | **Ich bezahle *bar/mit Kreditkarte*.** eekh beht·<u>sahl</u>·uh *bahr/miht* kreh·<u>deet</u>·kahrt·uh

> *i* At hotels, it is common to leave tips for services provided. If you are happy with the housekeeping service, leave a tip of €1–2 per day for the housekeeper in your room when you leave. Tip porters and your concierge €2–3 if they provide assistance.

Renting

I reserved *an apartment/a room*. | **Ich habe *ein Apartment/ein Zimmer* reserviert.** eekh <u>hahb</u>·uh *ien ah·<u>pahrt</u>·muhnt/ien <u>tsihm</u>·mehr* reh·sehr·<u>veert</u>

My name is... | **Mein Name ist ...** mien <u>nahm</u>·uh ihst ...

Can I have the keys? | **Kann ich den Schlüssel haben?** kahn eekh dehn <u>shlews</u>·suhl hah·buhn

Are there...? | **Gibt es ...?** gihpt ehs ...

– dishes | **– Geschirr** guh·<u>sheer</u>

– pillows | **– Kissen** <u>kihs</u>·suhn

– sheets | **– Bettwäsche** <u>beht</u>·vehsh·uh

– towels | **– Handtücher** <u>hahnt</u>·tewkh·ehr

– utensils | **– Haushaltsgeräte** <u>hows</u>·hahlts·guh·reht·uh

When do I put out the *trash [rubbish]/ recycling*?	**Wann stelle ich den *Abfall/Müll* raus?** vahn shtehl·luh eekh dehn *ahp·fahl/mewl* rows
...is broken.	**... funktioniert nicht.** ... foonk·syoh·neert neekht
How does...work?	**Wie funktioniert ...?** vee foonk·syoh·neert ...
– the air conditioner	**– die Klimaanlage** dee kleem·uh·ahn·lahg·uh
– the dishwasher	**– die Spülmaschine** dee shpewl·mah·sheen·uh
– the freezer	**– der Gefrierschrank** dehr guh·freer·shrahnk
– the heating	**– die Heizung** dee hiet·soong
– the microwave	**– die Mikrowelle** dee mee·kroh·vehl·luh
– the refrigerator	**– der Kühlschrank** dehr kewhl·shrahnk
– the stove	**– der Herd** dehr hehrd
– the washing machine	**– die Waschmaschine** dee vahsh·mah·shee·nuh

Household Items

I need...	**Ich brauche ...** eekh browkh·uh ...
– an adapter	**– einen Adapter** ien·uhn ah·dahp·tehr
– aluminum [kitchen] foil	**– Alufolie** ah·loo·foh·lee·uh
– a bottle opener	**– einen Flaschenöffner** ien·uhn flahsh·uhn·erf·nehr
– a broom	**– einen Besen** ien·uhn behz·uhn
– a can opener	**– einen Dosenöffner** ien·uhn doh·suhn·erf·nehr
– cleaning supplies	**– Reinigungsmittel** rien·ee·goongs·miht·tuhl
– a corkscrew	**– einen Korkenzieher** ien·uhn kohrk·uhn·tsee·ehr
– detergent	**– Waschmittel** vahsh·miht·tuhl
– dishwashing liquid	**– Geschirrspülmittel** guh·sheer·shpewl·miht·tuhl

– garbage [rubbish] bags	**– Abfallsäcke** <u>ahb</u>·fahl·seh·khuh
– a lightbulb	**– eine Glühbirne** <u>ien</u>·uh <u>glewh</u>·beer·nuh
– matches	**– Streichhölzer** <u>shtriekh</u>·herlt·sehr
– a mop	**– einen Wischmopp** <u>ien</u>·uhn <u>vihsh</u>·mohp
– napkins	**– Servietten** sehr·<u>vyeht</u>·tuhn
– paper towels	**– Küchenrollen** <u>kewkh</u>·uhn·rohl·luhn
– plastic wrap [cling film]	**– Frischhaltefolie** <u>frihsh</u>·hahl·tuh·foh·lee·uh
– a plunger	**– eine Saugglocke** <u>ien</u>·uh <u>zowg</u>·lohk·uh
– scissors	**– eine Schere** <u>ien</u>·uh <u>shehr</u>·uh
– a vacuum cleaner	**– einen Staubsauger** <u>ien</u>·uhn <u>shtowb</u>·sowg·ehr

▶ For dishes and utensils, see page 68.

▶ For oven temperatures, see page 174.

Hostel

Is there a bed available?	**Haben Sie ein Bett frei?** <u>hah</u>·buhn zee ien beht frie
Can I have…?	**Kann ich … haben?** kahn eekh … <u>hah</u>·buhn
– a *single/double* room	**– ein *Einzelzimmer/Doppelzimmer*** ien *<u>ient</u>·sehl·tsihm·mehr/<u>dohp</u>·pehl·tsihm·muhr*
– a blanket	**– eine Decke** <u>ien</u>·uh <u>dehk</u>·huh
– a pillow	**– ein Kissen** ien <u>kihs</u>·suhn
– sheets	**– Bettwäsche** <u>beht</u>·vehsh·uh
– a towel	**– ein Handtuch** ien <u>hahnt</u>·tookh
Do you have lockers?	**Haben Sie Schließfächer?** <u>hah</u>·buhn zee <u>shlees</u>·fehkh·ehr
When do you lock up?	**Wann schließen Sie ab?** vahn <u>shlees</u>·suhn zee ahp
Do I need a membership card?	**Brauche ich eine Mitgliedskarte?** <u>browkh</u>·uh eekh <u>ien</u>·uh <u>miht</u>·gleeds·kahrt·uh

Here's my international student card.	**Hier ist mein internationaler Studentenausweis.** heer ihst mien ihn·tehr·nah·syoh·<u>nahl</u>·ehr shtoo·<u>dehnt</u>·uhn·ows·vies

> *i*
>
> There are more than 500 hostels throughout Germany, in cities large and small and in rural locations. You may need a Hostelling International membership card to stay at these hostels, many of which belong to **Deutsches Jugendherbergswerk (DJV)**. Hostels are inexpensive accommodations that offer dormitory-style rooms and, sometimes, private or semi-private rooms. Some offer private bathrooms, though most have shared facilities. There is usually a self-service kitchen on-site. Booking in advance is a good idea, especially in large cities during festivals or holidays. Reservations can be made over the phone or online. Visit the Hostelling International website for more information.

Camping

Can I camp here?	**Kann ich hier campen?** kahn eekh heer <u>kahmp</u>·uhn
Where's the campsite?	**Wo ist der Campingplatz?** voh ihst dehr <u>kahmp</u>·eeng·plahts
What is the charge per *day/week*?	**Was kostet es pro *Tag/Woche*?** vahs <u>kohst</u>·uht ehs proh *tahk/<u>vohkh</u>·uh*
Are there…?	**Gibt es …?** gihpt ehs …
– cooking facilities	– **Kochmöglichkeiten** <u>kohkh</u>·merg·leekh·kiet·uhn
– electric outlets	– **Steckdosen** <u>shtehkh</u>·dohz·uhn
– laundry facilities	– **Waschmaschine** <u>vahsh</u>·maksch·een·uh
– showers	– **Duschen** <u>doosh</u>·uhn
– tents for rent [hire]	– **Mietzelte** <u>meet</u>·tsehl·tuh
Where can I empty the chemical toilet?	**Wo kann ich die Campingtoilette leeren?** voh kahn eekh dee <u>kahmp</u>·eeng·toy·leh·tuh <u>lehr</u>·uhn

You May See...

TRINKWASSER	drinking water
ZELTEN VERBOTEN	no camping
OFFENES FEUER VERBOTEN	no fires

▶ For household items, see page 46.

▶ For dishes and utensils, see page 68.

Internet and Communications

Essential

Where's an
internet cafe?
Wo gibt es ein Internetcafé? voh gihpt
ehs ien _ihnt_·ehr·neht·kah·_feh_

Can I *access the
internet/check
e-mail*?
**Kann ich *das Internet benutzen/meine
E-Mails lesen*?** kahn eekh *dahs _ihnt_·ehr·neht
beh·_noot_·suhn/_mien_·uh _ee_·miels _lehz_·uhn*

How much per
(half) hour?
Wie viel kostet eine (halbe) Stunde?
vee feel _kohst_·uht ien·uh (_hahlb_·uh) _shtoond_·uh

How do I log on?
Wie melde ich mich an? vee _mehld_·uh
eekh meekh ahn

A phone card,
please.
Eine Telefonkarte, bitte. ien·uh
tehl·uh·fohn·kahrt·uh _biht_·tuh

Can I have your
phone number?
Kann ich Ihre Telefonnummer haben?
kahn eekh _eehr_·uh tehl·uh·_fohn_·noom·ehr
hah·buhn

Here's my
number/e-mail.
Hier ist meine *Telefonnummer/E-Mail*.
heer ihst _mien_·uh *tehl·uh·_fohn_·noom·ehr/_ee_·miel*

Call me.
Rufen Sie mich an. _roo_·fuhn zee meekh ahn

E-mail me.
Mailen Sie mir. _miel_·uhn zee meer

Hello. This is…	**Hallo. Hier ist …** hah·loh heer ihst …
Can I speak to…?	**Kann ich mit … sprechen?** kahn eekh miht … shprehkh·uhn
Could you repeat that, please?	**Könnten Sie das bitte wiederholen?** kern·tuhn zee dahs biht·tuh veed·ehr·hohl·uhn
I'll call back later.	**Ich rufe später zurück.** eekh roof·uh shpeht·ehr tsoo·rewkh
Bye.	**Auf Wiederhören.** owf veed·ehr·her·ruhn
Where's the post office?	**Wo ist die Post?** voh ihst dee pohst
I'd like to send this to…	**Ich möchte das nach … schicken.** eekh merkh·tuh dahs nahkh … shihk·uhn

Computer, Internet and E-mail

Where's an internet cafe?	**Wo gibt es ein Internetcafé?** voh gihpt ehs ien ihnt·ehr·neht·kah·feh
Does it have wireless internet?	**Gibt es dort wireless Internet?** gihpt ehs dohrt wier·luhs ihnt·ehr·neht
How do I turn the computer *on/off*?	**Wie schalte ich den Computer *an/aus*?** vee shahlt·uh eekh dehn kohm·pjoot·ehr *ahn/ows*
Can I…?	**Kann ich …?** kahn eekh …
– access the internet	– **das Internet benutzen** dahs ihnt·ehr·neht beh·noot·suhn
– check e-mail	– **E-Mails lesen** ee·miels lehz·uhn
– print	– **drucken** drook·uhn
– use any computer	– **einen Computer benutzen** ien·uhn kohm·pjoot·ehr beh·noot·suhn
How much per (half) hour?	**Wie viel kostet eine (halbe) Stunde?** vee feel kohst·uht ien·uh (hahlb·uh) shtoond·uh

How...?	**Wie ...?** vee ...
– do I connect	**– stelle ich eine Verbindung her** shteh·luh eekh ien·uh fuhr·bihnd·oong hehr
– do I disconnect	**– trenne ich eine Verbindung** trehn·uh eekh ien·uh fuhr·bihnd·oong
– do I log *on/off*	**– melde ich mich *an/ab*** mehld·uh eekh meekh *ahn/ahp*
– do I type this symbol	**– gebe ich dieses Zeichen ein** geh·buh eekh deez·uhs tsiekh·ehn ien
What's your e-mail?	**Wie ist Ihre E-Mail-Adresse?** vee ihst eehr·uh ee·miel·ah·drehs·uh
My e-mail is...	**Meine E-Mail-Adresse ist ...** mien·uh ee·miel·ah·drehs·uh ihst ...

You May See...

SCHLIESSEN	close
LÖSCHEN	delete
E-MAIL	e-mail
BEENDEN	exit
HILFE	help
INSTANT MESSENGER	instant messenger
INTERNET	internet
ANMELDEN	login
NEUE NACHRICHT	new message
AN/AUS	on/off
ÖFFNEN	open
DRUCKEN	print
SPEICHERN	save
SENDEN	send
BENUTZERNAME/PASSWORT	username/password
WIRELESS INTERNET	wireless internet

Phone

A phone card, please.	**Eine Telefonkarte, bitte.** <u>ien</u>·uh tehl·eh·<u>fohn</u>·kahrt·uh <u>biht</u>·tuh
An international phonecard for...	**Eine internationale Telefonkarte für ...** <u>ien</u>·uh ihnt·ehr·nah·syoh·<u>nahl</u>·uh tehl·uh·<u>fohn</u>·kahrt·uh fewr ...
– Australia	**– Australien** ow·<u>shtrah</u>·lee·ehn
– Canada	**– Kanada** <u>kah</u>·nah·dah
– Ireland	**– Irland** <u>eer</u>·lahnt

– the U.K.	**– Großbritannien** grohs·bree·<u>tahn</u>·ee·ehn
– the U.S.	**– die USA** dee <u>oo</u>·ehs·ah
How much?	**Wie viel kostet es?** vee feel <u>kohs</u>·tuht ehs
Can I recharge this phone?	**Kann ich dieses Telefon wieder aufladen?** kahn eekh <u>deez</u>·uhs tehl·uh·<u>fohn</u> <u>veed</u>·ehr owf·<u>lahd</u>·uhn
My phone doesn't work here.	**Mein Telefon funktioniert hier nicht.** mien tehl·leh·<u>fohn</u> foonk·syoh·<u>neert</u> heer neekht
What's the *area code/country code* for…?	**Was ist die *Ortsvorwahl/Landesvorwahl* für …?** vahs ihst dee *<u>ohrts</u>·fohr·vahl/ lahnd·uhs·fohr·vahl* fewr …
What's the number for Information?	**Was ist die Nummer für die Auskunft?** vahs ihst dee <u>noom</u>·ehr fewr dee <u>ows</u>·kuhnft
I'd like the number for…	**Ich hätte gern die Nummer für …** eekh <u>heht</u>·uh gehrn dee <u>noom</u>·ehr fewr …
I'd like to call collect [reverse the charges].	**Ich möchte ein R-Gespräch führen.** eekh <u>merkh</u>·tuh ien <u>ehr</u>·guh·shprehkh <u>fewhr</u>·uhn
Can I have your number, please?	**Können Sie mir bitte Ihre Nummer geben?** <u>kern</u>·uhn zee meer <u>biht</u>·tuh <u>eehr</u>·uh <u>noom</u>·ehr <u>gehb</u>·uhn
Here's my number.	**Hier ist meine Nummer.** heer ihst <u>mien</u>·uh <u>noom</u>·ehr

▶ For numbers, see page 167.

Please call me.	**Bitte rufen Sie mich an.** <u>biht</u>·tuh <u>roof</u>·uhn zee meekh ahn
Please text me.	**Bitte schicken Sie mir eine SMS.** bit·tuh <u>shihk</u>·uhn zee meer <u>ien</u>·uh <u>ehs</u>·ehm·ehs

| I'll call you. | **Ich werde Sie anrufen.** eekh <u>vehrd</u>·uh zee <u>ahn</u>·roof·uhn |
| I'll text you. | **Ich werde Ihnen eine SMS schicken.** eekh <u>vehrd</u>·uh <u>eehn</u>·uhn <u>ien</u>·uh <u>ehs</u>·ehm·ehs <u>shihk</u>·uhn |

On the Phone

Hello. This is…	**Hallo. Hier ist …** <u>hahl</u>·loh heer ihst …
Can I speak to…?	**Kann ich mit … sprechen?** kahn eekh miht … <u>shprehkh</u>·uhn
Extension…	**Durchwahl …** <u>doorkh</u>·vahl …
Speak *louder/more slowly*, please.	**Bitte sprechen Sie *lauter/langsamer*.** <u>biht</u>·tuh <u>shprehkh</u>·uhn zee *<u>lowt</u>·ehr/<u>lahng</u>·sahm·ehr*
Could you repeat that, please?	**Könnten Sie das bitte wiederholen?** <u>kern</u>·tuhn zee dahs <u>biht</u>·tuh vee·dehr·<u>hohl</u>·uhn
I'll call back later.	**Ich rufe später zurück.** eekh <u>roof</u>·uh <u>shpeht</u>·ehr tsoo·<u>rewkh</u>
Bye.	**Auf Wiederhören.** owf <u>veed</u>·ehr·her·ruhn

▶For business travel, see page 139.

You May Hear...

Ruff an? roof ahn

Who's calling?

Einen Moment, bitte. ien·uhn moh·mehnt biht·tuh

Hold on, please.

Ich verbinde Sie. eekh fehr·bihnd·uh zee

I'll put you through.

Er♂/Sie♀ ist nicht da/spricht gerade. ehr♂/zee♀ ihst neekht dah/shpreekht geh·rahd·uh

He/She is *not here/ on another line.*

Möchten Sie eine Nachricht hinterlassen? merkh·tuhn zee ien·uh nahkh·reekht hihnt·ehr·lahs·suhn

Would you like to leave a message?

Bitte rufen Sie *später/in zehn Minuten* zurück. biht·tuh roof·uhn zee *shpeht·ehr/ihn tsehn* mee·noot·uhn tsoo·rewkh

Please call back *later/in ten minutes.*

Kann er♂/sie♀ zurückrufen? khan ehr♂/zee♀ tsoo·rewkh·roof·uhn

Can he/she call you back?

Was ist Ihre Nummer? vahs ihst eehr·uh noom·ehr

What's your number?

Fax

Can I *send/receive* a fax here?

Kann ich hier ein Fax *senden/ empfangen*? kahn eekh heer ien fahks *zehnd·uhn/ehm·pfahng·uhn*

What's the fax number?

Was ist die Faxnummer? vahs ihst dee fahks·noom·ehr

Please fax this to...

Bitte faxen Sie das nach ... biht·tuh fahks·uhn zee dahs nahkh ...

i German public phones are mainly card operated. Phone cards in various amounts can be purchased at newsstands, supermarkets and other shops.

Important telephone numbers include:
Police 110
Fire 112
Ambulance 115
National Directory 11833
National Directory (in English) 11837
International Directory 11834

To call the U.S. or Canada from Germany, dial 00 + 1 + area code + phone number. To call the U.K. from Germany, dial 00 + 44 + area code (minus the first 0) + phone number.

Post Office

Where's the *post office/mailbox [postbox]*?	**Wo ist *die Post/der Briefkasten*?** voh ihst dee pohst/dehr *breef·kahs·tuhn*
A stamp for this *postcard/letter* to…, please.	**Eine Briefmarke für *diese Postkarte/diesen Brief* nach … bitte.** *ien*·uh breef·mahrk·uh fewr *deez·uh pohst·kahrt·uh/ deez·uhn* breef nahkh … biht·tuh
How much?	**Wie viel kostet das?** vee feel kohs·tuht dahs
Please send this package *by airmail/ express.*	**Senden Sie dieses Paket bitte per *Luftpost/Express.*** zehnd·uhn zee *deez*·uhs pah·*keht* biht·tuh pehr *looft·pohst/ehks·prehs*
A receipt, please.	**Eine Quittung, bitte.** *ien*·uh *kveet*·toong *biht*·tuh

You May Hear...

Bitte füllen Sie das Zollformular aus.
biht·tuh fewl·luhn zee dahs
tsohl·fohr·moo·lahr ows

Fill out the customs
declaration form,
please.

Wie viel ist es wert? vee feel ihst ehs vehrt

What's the value?

Was ist der Inhalt? vahs ihst dehr ihn·hahlt

What's inside?

---

i

In addition to mailing options, German post offices offer a
variety of other services. Most provide banking services and
allow you to deposit or withdraw money and apply for a credit
card. On weekdays, post offices are usually open from
8:30 a.m. to 1 p.m., and again from 2:30 p.m. to 4 p.m.
(in larger cities to 6:30 p.m.). On Saturdays they are open
from 8:30 a.m. to 1 p.m.

▼ *Food*

Eating Out

Essential

Can you recommend a good *restaurant/ bar*?	**Können Sie *ein gutes Restaurant/eine gute Bar* empfehlen?** ker·nuhn zee *ien goo·*tuhs reh·stow·rahnt/*ien·*uh goo·tuh bahr ehm·pfeh·luhn
Is there a *traditional German/inexpensive* restaurant nearby?	**Gibt es in der Nähe ein *typisch deutsches/ preisgünstiges* Restaurant?** gihpt ehs ihn dehr neh·uh ien *tew·peesh doy·chuhs/ pries·gewn·stee·guhs* reh·stow·rahnt
A table for…, please.	**Bitte einen Tisch für …** biht·tuh ien·uhn tihsh fewr …
Can we sit…?	**Können wir … sitzen?** ker·nuhn veer … ziht·tsuhn
– here/there	**– hier/dort** heer/dohrt
– outside	**– draußen** drow·suhn
– in a non-smoking area	**– in einem Nichtraucherbereich** ihn ien·uhm neekht·row·khehr·beh·riehk
I'm waiting for someone.	**Ich warte auf jemanden.** eekh vahr·tuh owf yeh·mahnd·uhn
Where's the restroom [toilet]?	**Wo ist die Toilette?** voh ihst dee toy·leh·tuh
A menu, please.	**Die Speisekarte, bitte.** dee shpie·zuh·kahr·tuh biht·tuh
What do you recommend?	**Was empfehlen Sie?** vahs ehm·pfeh·luhn zee
I'd like…	**Ich möchte …** eekh merkh·tuh …
Some more…, please.	**Etwas mehr …, bitte.** eht·vahs mehr … biht·tuh
Enjoy your meal!	**Guten Appetit!** goo·tuhn ah·puh·teet

The check [bill], please.	**Die Rechnung, bitte.** dee <u>rehkh</u>·noonk <u>biht</u>·tuh
Is service included?	**Ist die Bedienung im Preis enthalten?** ihsht dee buh·<u>dee</u>·nung ihm pries <u>ehnt</u>·hahl·tuhn
Can I pay *by credit card/have a receipt*?	**Kann ich *mit Kreditkarte bezahlen/eine Quittung haben*?** kahn eekh *miht kreh·<u>deet</u>·kahr·tuh beht·<u>sahl</u>·uhn/<u>ien</u>·uh <u>kvee</u>·toonk hah·buhn*
Thank you!	**Danke!** <u>dahn</u>·kuh

Restaurant Types

Can you recommend...?	**Können Sie ... empfehlen?** <u>ker</u>·nuhn zee ... ehm·<u>pfeh</u>·luhn
– a restaurant	**– ein Restaurant** ien reh·stow·<u>rahnt</u>
– a bar	**– eine Bar** <u>ien</u>·uh bahr
– a cafe	**– ein Café** ien kah·<u>feh</u>
– a fast-food place	**– ein Schnellrestaurant** ien <u>shnehl</u>·reh·stow·rahnt
– a snack bar	**– einen Imbiss** <u>ien</u>·uhn <u>ihm</u>·bees

> **Das Frühstück** (breakfast) can range from a large meal, usually served buffet style, to a simple dish of bread, jam and butter. **Das Mittagessen** (lunch), typically a large and heavy meal, is normally served from 12:00 to 2:00 p.m. In larger cities, many Germans will have lunch at a beer garden or hall with cafeteria-style service. **Das Abendessen** (dinner) is served from 6:00 to 9:00 p.m. and is usually a light meal.

Reservations and Questions

I'd like to reserve a table…	**Ich möchte einen Tisch … reservieren** eekh merkh·tuh ien·uhn tihsh … reh·zuh·veer·ehn
– for two	**– für zwei Personen** fewr tsvie pehr·zohn·uhn
– for this evening	**– für heute Abend** fewr hoy·tuh ah·behnt
– for tomorrow at…	**– für morgen um …** fewr mohr·guhn oom …
A table for two, please.	**Bitte einen Tisch für zwei.** biht·tuh ien·uhn tihsh fewr tsvie
We have a reservation.	**Wir haben eine Reservierung.** veer hah·buhn ien·uh reh·zuh·veer·uhng
My name is…	**Mein Name ist …** mien nahm·uh ihst …
Can we sit…?	**Können wir … sitzen?** ker·nuhn veer … ziht·tsuhn
– here/there	**– hier/dort** heer/dohrt
– outside	**– draußen** drow·suhn
– in a non-smoking area	**– in einem Nichtraucherbereich** ihn ien·uhm neekht·row·kluhr·beh·riekh
– by the window	**– am Fenster** ahm fehn·stehr
Where's the restroom [toilet]?	**Wo ist die Toilette?** voh ihst dee toy·leh·tuh

You May Hear...

Haben Sie eine Reservierung? hah·buhn zee ien·uh reh·zuh·<u>veer</u>·uhng

Do you have a reservation?

Für wie viele Personen? fewr vee <u>fee</u>·luh pehr·<u>zohn</u>·uhn

For how many people?

Raucher oder Nichtraucher? <u>row</u>·khuhr <u>oh</u>·duhr <u>neekht</u>·row·khuhr

Smoking or non-smoking?

Möchten Sie jetzt bestellen? <u>merkh</u>·tuhn zee yehtst buh·<u>shteh</u>·luhn

Are you ready to order?

Was möchten Sie? vahs <u>merkh</u>·tuhn zee

What would you like?

Ich empfehle ... eekh ehm·<u>pfeh</u>·luh ...

I recommend...

Guten Appetit. <u>goo</u>·tuhn ah·puh·<u>teet</u>

Enjoy your meal.

Ordering

Waiter/Waitress!

Bedienung! buh·<u>dee</u>·nounk

We're ready to order.

Wir möchten bitte bestellen. weer <u>merkh</u>·tuhn <u>biht</u>·tuh buh·<u>shteh</u>·luhn

The wine list, please.

Die Weinkarte, bitte. dee <u>vien</u>·kahr·tuh <u>biht</u>·tuh

I'd like...

Ich möchte ... eekh <u>merhk</u>·tuh ...

– a bottle of...

– eine Flasche ... <u>ien</u>·uh <u>flah</u>·shuh ...

– a carafe of...

– eine Karaffe ... <u>ien</u>·uh kah·<u>rah</u>·fuh ...

– a glass of...

– ein Glas ... ien glahs ...

▶ For alcoholic and non-alcoholic drinks, see page 80.

The menu, please.

Die Speisekarte, bitte. dee <u>shpie</u>·zuh·kahr·tuh <u>biht</u>·tuh

Do you have…?	**Haben Sie …?** <u>hah</u>·buhn zee …
– a menu in English	**– eine Speisekarte in Englisch** <u>ien</u>·uh <u>shpie</u>·zuh·kahr·tuh ihn <u>ehn</u>·gleesh
– a fixed-price menu	**– ein Festpreismenü** ien <u>fehst</u>·pries·meh·new
– a children's menu	**– ein Kindermenü** ien <u>kihn</u>·dehr·meh·new
What do you recommend?	**Was empfehlen Sie?** vahs ehm·<u>pfeh</u>·luhn zee
What's this?	**Was ist das?** vahs ihsht dahs
What's in it?	**Was ist darin?** vahs ihsht dah·<u>rihn</u>
Is it spicy?	**Ist es scharf?** ihsht ehs shahrf
Without…, please.	**Ohne …, bitte.** <u>oh</u>·nuh … <u>biht</u>·tuh
It's to go [take away], please.	**Bitte zum Mitnehmen.** <u>biht</u>·tuh tsoom <u>miht</u>·neh·muhn

You May See…

SPEISEKARTE	menu
TAGESMENÜ	menu of the day
SPEZIALITÄTEN	specials

Cooking Methods

baked	**gebacken** guh·<u>bahkh</u>·uhn
boiled	**gekocht** guh·<u>kohkht</u>
braised	**geschmort** guh·<u>shmohrt</u>
breaded	**paniert** pah·<u>neert</u>
creamed	**püriert** <u>pew</u>·reert
diced	**gewürfelt** guh·<u>vewr</u>·fuhlt
fileted	**filetiert** fee·luh·<u>teert</u>

fried	**gebraten** guh·<u>brah</u>·tuhn
grilled	**gegrillt** guh·<u>grihlt</u>
poached	**pochiert** <u>poh</u>·sheert
roasted	**geröstet** guh·<u>rer</u>·stuht
sautéed	**sautiert** <u>zow</u>·teert
smoked	**geräuchert** guh·<u>roy</u>·khuhrt
steamed	**gedünstet** guh·<u>dewn</u>·stuht
stewed	**geschmort** guh·<u>shmohrt</u>
stuffed	**gefüllt** guh·<u>fewlt</u>

Special Requirements

I'm…	**Ich bin …** eekh bihn …
– diabetic	**– Diabetiker** dee·ah·<u>beh</u>·tee·kehr
– vegetarian	**– Vegetarier** veh·guh·<u>tah</u>·ree·ehr
– vegan	**– Veganer** <u>veh</u>·gah·nehr
I'm allergic to…	**Ich bin allergisch auf …** eekh bihn ah·<u>lehr</u>·geesh owf …
I can't eat…	**Ich kann … essen.** eekh kahn … <u>eh</u>·zuhn
– dairy	**– keine Milchprodukte** <u>kien</u>·uh meelkh·proh·dook·tuh
– gluten	**– kein Gluten** kien <u>gloo</u>·tuhn
– nuts	**– keine Nüsse** <u>kien</u>·uh <u>new</u>·suh
– pork	**– kein Schweinefleisch** kien <u>shvie</u>·nuh·fliesh
– shellfish	**– keine Schalentiere** <u>kien</u>·uh <u>shah</u>·luhn·tee·ruh
– spicy foods	**– keine scharf gewürzten Speisen** <u>kien</u>·uh shahrf guh·<u>vewrt</u>·stuhn <u>shpie</u>·zuhn
– wheat	**– kein Weizen** kien <u>vie</u>·tsuhn
Is it *halal/kosher*?	**Ist es *halal/koscher*?** ihsht ehs hah·<u>lahl</u>/ <u>koh</u>·shuhr

Dining with Kids

Do you have children's portions?	**Haben Sie Kinderportionen?** hah·buhn zee kihn·dehr·pohr·syoh·nuhn
A *highchair/child's seat*, please.	**Einen *Kindersitz/Kinderstuhl*, bitte.** ien·uhn kihnd·ehr·zihtz/kihn·dehr·shtuhl biht·tuh
Where can I *feed/change* the baby?	**Wo kann ich das Baby *füttern/wickeln*?** voh kahn eekh dahs beh·bee few·tuhrn/vihk·uhln
Can you warm this?	**Können Sie das warm machen?** ker·nuhn zee dahs vahrm mah·khuhn

▶ For travel with children, see page 142.

Complaints

How much longer will our food be?	**Wie lange dauert es noch mit dem Essen?** vee lahng·uh dow·ehrt ehs nohkh miht dehm eh·suhn
We can't wait any longer.	**Wir können nicht mehr länger warten.** veer ker·nuhn neekht mehr lehng·ehr vahr·tuhn
We're leaving.	**Wir gehen jetzt.** veer geh·ehn yehtst
I didn't order this.	**Das habe ich nicht bestellt.** dahs hah·buh eekh neekht buh·shtehlt
I ordered...	**Ich habe ... bestellt.** eekh hah·buh ... buh·shtehlt
I can't eat this.	**Ich kann das nicht essen.** eekh kahn dahs neekht eh·suhn
This is too...	**Das ist zu ...** dahs ihst tsoo ...
– cold/hot	**– kalt/heiß** kahlt/hies
– salty/spicy	**– salzig/scharf gewürzt** sahl·tseek/shahrf guh·vewrts
– tough/bland	**– zäh/fad** tseh/fahd
This isn't *clean/fresh*.	**Das ist nicht *sauber/frisch*.** dahs ihst neekht zow·buhr/frihsh

Paying

The check [bill], please.	**Die Rechnung, bitte.** dee <u>rehkh</u>·noonk <u>biht</u>·tuh
Separate checks [bills], please.	**Getrennte Rechungen, bitte.** geh·<u>trehn</u>·tuh <u>rehkh</u>·noong·uhn <u>biht</u>·tuh
It's all together.	**Alles zusammen.** <u>ah</u>·luhs tsoo·<u>zah</u>·muhn
Is service included?	**Ist die Bedienung im Preis enthalten?** ihsht dee buh·<u>dee</u>·noonk ihm pries ehnt·<u>hahl</u>·tuhn
What's this amount for?	**Wofür ist diese Summe?** <u>voh</u>·fewr ihsht dee·zuh <u>soo</u>·muh
I didn't have that. I had…	**Das hatte ich nicht. Ich hatte …** dahs <u>hah</u>·tuh eekh neekht eekh <u>hah</u>·tuh …
Can I…?	**Kann ich …?** kahn eekh …
– pay with credit card	**– mit Kreditkarte bezahlen** miht kreh·<u>deet</u>·kahr·tuh beht·<u>sahl</u>·uhn
– have a receipt	**– eine Quittung haben** <u>ien</u>·uh <u>kvee</u>·toonk <u>hah</u>·buhn
– have an itemized bill	**– eine aufgeschlüsselte Rechnung haben** <u>ien</u>·uh <u>owf</u>·guh·shlew·sehl·tuh <u>rehkh</u>·oong·uhn <u>hah</u>·buhn
That was delicious!	**Das war lecker!** dahs vahr <u>leh</u>·khehr

---

i Service is included in German restaurants and bars, as is value added tax (VAT). However, it is still typical to leave a small tip; round to the nearest euro or two for a small bill or add 5–10%, rounding to a full euro, for a larger bill. Note that it is not typical to be given a check. The server will usually just tell you your total, and you will hand the money to the server, specifying how much change you need back (so the tip is included, not left on the table later).

Market

Where are the *carts [trolleys]/baskets*?	**Wo sind die *Einkaufswagen/Einkaufskörbe*?** voh zihnt dee <u>ien</u>·kowfs·vah·guhn/<u>ien</u>·kowfs·kehr·buh
Where is…?	**Wo ist …?** voh ihsht …

▶ For food items, see page 84.

I'd like some of *that/this.*	**Ich möchte etwas von *dem/diesem*.** eekh <u>merkh</u>·tuh <u>eht</u>·vahs fohn *dehm/<u>dee</u>·zuhm*
Can I taste it?	**Kann ich es kosten?** kahn eekh ehs <u>kohs</u>·tuhn
I'd like…	**Ich möchte …** eekh <u>merkh</u>·tuh …
– a kilo/half-kilo of…	**– ein *Kilo/halbes Kilo* …** ien <u>kee</u>·loh/<u>hahl</u>·buhs <u>kee</u>·loh …
– a liter of…	**– einen Liter …** <u>ien</u>·uhn <u>lee</u>·tehr …
– a piece of…	**– ein Stück …** ien shtewk …
– a slice of…	**– eine Scheibe …** <u>ien</u>·uh <u>shie</u>·buh …
More./Less.	**Mehr./Weniger.** mehr/<u>veh</u>·nee·guhr
How much?	**Wie viel kostet das?** vee feel <u>kohs</u>·tuht dahs
Where do I pay?	**Wo bezahle ich?** voh beht·<u>sahl</u>·uh eekh
A bag, please.	**Eine Tüte, bitte.** <u>ien</u>·uh <u>tew</u>·tuh <u>biht</u>·tuh
I'm being helped.	**Ich werde schon bedient.** eekh <u>vehr</u>·duh shohn buh·<u>deent</u>

▶ For conversion tables, see page 173.

You May Hear…

Kann ich Ihnen helfen? kahn eekh <u>eehn</u>·uhn <u>hehl</u>·fuhn	Can I help you?
Was möchten Sie? vahs <u>merkh</u>·tuhn zee	What would you like?
Noch etwas? nohkh <u>eht</u>·vahs	Anything else?
Das macht … Euro. dahs mahkht … <u>oy</u>·roh	That's…euros.

> *i*
>
> Local markets that sell fresh produce and homemade goods can be found in most cities throughout Germany. The days and hours of operation vary widely. Your hotel concierge or a tourist information office can provide details.

You May See...

MINDESTENS HALTBAR BIS ...	best before...
KALORIEN	calories
FETTARM	low fat
GEKÜHLT LAGERN	keep refrigerated
KANN SPUREN VON ... BEINHALTEN	may contain traces of...
MIKROWELLENGEEIGNET	microwaveable
FÜR VEGETARIER GEEIGNET	suitable for vegetarians

Dishes, Utensils and Kitchen Tools

bottle opener	**der Flaschenöffner** dehr flah·shuhn·erf·nehr
bowl	**die Schüssel** dee shew·suhl
can opener	**der Dosenöffner** dehr doh·zuhn·erf·nuhr
corkscrew	**der Korkenzieher** dehr kohr·kuhn·tsee·uhr
cup	**die Tasse** dee tah·suh
fork	**die Gabel** dee gah·buhl
frying pan	**die Bratpfanne** dee braht·pfah·nuh
glass	**das Glas** dahs glahs
(steak) knife	**das (Steak-) Messer** dahs (shtehk·) meh·sehr
measuring cup	**der Messbecher** dehr mehs·beh·khuhr
measuring spoon	**der Messlöffel** dehr mehs·ler·fuhl
napkin	**die Serviette** dee sehr·vyeh·tuh
plate	**der Teller** dehr teh·lehr

pot	**der Topf** dehr tohpf
spatula	**der Spatel** dehr shpah·tuhl
spoon	**der Löffel** dehr ler·fuhl

Meals

Breakfast

der Apfelsaft dehr ah·pfuhl·zahft	apple juice
der Aufschnitt dehr owf·shnihl	cold cuts [charcuterie]
das Brot dahs broht	bread
das Brötchen dahs brert·khuhn	roll
die Butter dee boo·tehr	butter
das ... Ei dahs ... ie	...egg
– *hart/weich* **gekochte** *hahrt/viekh* guh·kohkh·tuh	– *hard-/soft-*boiled
der Joghurt dehr yoh·goort	yogurt
der *Kaffee/Tee* ... dehr *kah·feh/tee* ...	coffee/tea...
– **entkoffeiniert** ehnt·koh·feh·een·eert	– decaf
– **mit Milch** miht mihlkh	– with milk
– **mit Süßstoff** miht zews·shtohf	– with artificial sweetener
– **mit Zucker** miht tsoo·khuhr	– with sugar
– **schwarz** shvahrts	– black

I'd like...	**Ich möchte gern ...** eekh merkh·tuh gehrn ...
More..., please.	**Mehr ..., bitte.** mehr ... biht·tuh
With/Without...	**Mit/Ohne ...** miht/oh·nuh ...
I can't have...	**Ich vertrage *kein/keine* ...** eekh fehr·trah·guh *kien/kien*·uh ...

▶ For when to use **kein** or **keine**, see page 164.

der Käse dehr <u>kay</u>·zuh	cheese
der Kräutertee dehr <u>krow</u>·tehr·tee	herbal tea
die Marmelade dee mahr·muh·<u>lah</u>·duh	jam/jelly
die Milch dee mihlkh	milk
der Muffin dehr <u>moo</u>·fihn	muffin
das Müsli dahs <u>mew</u>·slee	granola [muesli]
das Omelett dahs <u>ohm</u>·luht	omelet
der Orangensaft dehr oh·<u>rahng</u>·uhn·zahft	orange juice
der Pampelmusensaft dehr pahm·puhl·<u>moo</u>·zuhn·zahft	grapefruit juice
das Rührei dahs <u>rew</u>·rie	scrambled egg
der Saft dehr zahft	juice
der Schinken dehr <u>shihn</u>·kuhn	ham
das Spiegelei dahs <u>shpeeg</u>·uh·lie	fried egg
der Toast dehr tohst	toast
das Wasser dahs <u>vah</u>·sehr	water

Appetizers [Starters]

die Appetithäppchen dee ah·peh·<u>teet</u>·hehp·khehn	finger sandwiches
die Aufschnittplatte dee <u>owf</u>·shniht·plah·tuh	cold cuts served with bread
der Bismarckhering dehr <u>bees</u>·mahrk·heh·reeng	marinated herring with onions

I'd like…	**Ich möchte gern …** eekh <u>merkh</u>·tuh gehrn …
More…, please.	**Mehr …, bitte.** mehr … <u>biht</u>·tuh …
With/Without…	**Mit/Ohne …** miht/<u>oh</u>·nuh …

die Fleischpastete dee _fliesh_·pah·steh·tuh	meat pâté
die Gänseleberpastete dee gehn·zehl·_leh_·behr·pah·steh·tuh	goose liver pâté
die gefüllten Champignons dee geh·_fewl_·tehn _shahm_·pee·nyohns	stuffed mushrooms
der gemischte Salat dehr _geh_·meesh·tuh sah·_laht_	mixed salad
die Käseplatte dee _kay_·zuh·plah·tuh	cheese platter
das Knoblauchbrot dahs _knoh_·blowkh·broht	garlic bread
der Krabbencocktail dehr _krahb_·behn·kohk·tayl	shrimp cocktail
die russischen Eier dee _roo_·see·shuh ier	hard-boiled eggs with mayonnaise
der Räucherlachs dehr _roy_·khurt·lahks	smoked salmon
der Salat dehr sah·_laht_	salad
die Soleier dee soh·_lier_	eggs boiled in brine
der Tomatensalat dehr _toh_·mah·tehn·sah·laht	tomato salad
der Wurstsalat dehr _voorst_·sah·laht	cold cuts with onion and oil

Soup

die Backerbsensuppe dee _bahk_·ehrbs·ehn·zoo·puh	broth with crisp, round noodles
die Bohnensuppe dee _boh_·nuhn·zoo·puh	bean soup

I can't have…	**Ich vertrage _kein/keine_ …** eekh fehr·_trah_·guh _kien/kien_·uh …

▶ For when to use **kein** or **keine**, see page 164.

die Champignoncremesuppe dee <u>shahm</u>·pee·nyohn·krehm·zoo·puh	cream of mushroom soup
die Erbsensuppe dee <u>ehrb</u>·zuhn·zoo·puh	pea soup
die Fleischbrühe dee <u>fliesh</u>·brew·uh	bouillon
die Frittatensuppe dee free·<u>tah</u>·tehn·zoo·puh	broth with pancake strips
die Frühlingssuppe dee <u>frew</u>·leeng·zoo·puh	spring vegetable soup
die Gemüsesuppe dee guh·<u>mew</u>·zuh·zoo·puh	vegetable soup
die Gulaschsuppe dee <u>gool</u>·ahsh·zoo·puh	stewed beef in a spicy soup
die Hühnersuppe dee <u>hewn</u>·ehr·zoo·puh	chicken soup
die klare Gemüsebrühe dee <u>klah</u>·ruh geh·<u>mew</u>·zuh·brew·uh	vegetable broth
die Linsensuppe dee <u>leen</u>·zehn·zoo·puh	lentil soup
die Semmelknödelsuppe dee <u>zeh</u>·mehl·kner·dehl·zoo·puh	bread dumpling soup
die Tomatensuppe dee toh·<u>mah</u>·tuhn·zoo·puh	tomato soup
die Zwiebelsuppe dee <u>tsvee</u>·behl·zoo·puh	onion soup

Fish and Seafood

der Aal dehr ahl	eel
die Auster dee <u>ow</u>·stehr	oyster
die Brachse dee <u>brahk</u>·suh	bream
der Barsch dehr bahrsh	perch

I'd like…	**Ich möchte gern …** eekh <u>merkh</u>·tuh gehrn …
More…, please.	**Mehr …, bitte.** mehr … <u>biht</u>·tuh
With/Without…	**Mit/Ohne …** miht/<u>oh</u>·nuh …

der Brathering dehr brah·theh·reeng	fried sour herring
der Dorsch dehr dohrsh	cod
die Forelle dee foh·reh·luh	trout
die Garnele dee gahr·neh·luh	shrimp
der Heilbutt dehr hiel·boot	halibut
der Hering dehr heh·rihng	herring
der Hummer dehr hoo·mehr	lobster
der Krebs dehr krehbs	crab
der Lachs dehr lahks	salmon
die Makrele dee mah·kreh·luh	mackerel
die Muschel dee moo·shuhl	clam
der Oktopus dehr ohk·toh·poos	octopus
die Sardelle dee sahr·deh·luh	anchovy
die Sardine dee zahr·dee·nuh	sardine
die Scholle dee shoh·luh	flounder
der Schwertfisch dehr shvehrt·fihsh	swordfish
der Seebarsch dehr zeh·bahrsh	sea bass
die Seezunge dee zeh·tsoong·uh	sole
der Tintenfisch dehr tihn·tuhn·fihsh	squid
der Thunfisch dehr toon·fihsh	tuna

Meat and Poultry

die Berliner Buletten dee behr·lee·nuh boo·leh·tehn	fried meatballs, a specialty of Berlin
der Braten dehr brah·tuhn	roast

I can't have…	**Ich vertrage *kein/keine* …** eekh fehr·trah·guh *kien/kien·uh* …

▶ For when to use **kein** or **keine**, see page 164.

die Bratwurst dee <u>braht</u>·voorst	fried sausage
die Ente dee <u>ehn</u>·tuh	duck
das Filet dahs <u>fee</u>·leh	filet
der Fleischkäse dehr <u>fliesh</u>·kay·zuh	a kind of meatloaf
die Frikadelle dee free·kah·<u>dehl</u>·luh	fried meatballs
das Gulasch dahs <u>gool</u>·ahsh	stewed beef with spicy paprika gravy
der Hackbraten dehr <u>hahk</u>·brah·tuhn	meatloaf
das Hackfleisch dahs <u>hahk</u>·fliesh	ground meat
das Hühnchen dahs <u>hewn</u>·khuhn	chicken
das Spanferkel dahs <u>shpahn</u>·fehr·kehl	crunchy roasted suckling pig
das Kalbfleisch dahs <u>kahlb</u>·fliesh	veal
das Kaninchen dahs kah·<u>nihn</u>·khehn	rabbit

I'd like…	**Ich möchte gern …** eekh <u>merkh</u>·tuh gehrn …
More…, please.	**Mehr …, bitte.** mehr … <u>biht</u>·tuh
With/Without…	**Mit/Ohne …** miht/<u>oh</u>·nuh …

74

das Kotelett dahs koht·<u>leht</u>	pork chop
das Lamm dahs lahm	lamb
die Leber dee <u>leh</u>·behr	liver
die Niere dee <u>nee</u>·ruh	kidney
das Pökelfleisch dahs <u>pehr</u>·kehl·fliesh	pickled meat
der Rinderbraten dehr <u>reen</u>·dehr·brah·tuhn	roast beef
das Rindfleisch dahs <u>rihnt</u>·fliesh	beef
die Rouladen dee roo·<u>lah</u>·dehn	stuffed beef slices, rolled and braised in brown gravy
der Sauerbraten dehr <u>zow</u>·ehr·brah·tuhn	beef roast, marinated with herbs, in a rich sauce
der Schinken dehr <u>shihn</u>·kuhn	ham
der Schinkenspeck dehr <u>shihn</u>·kuhn·shpehk	bacon
das Schmorfleisch dahs <u>shmohr</u>·fliesh	stewed meat
das Schweinefleisch dahs <u>shvien</u>·uh·fliesh	pork
der Schweinebraten dehr <u>shvien</u>·brah·tuhn	roast pork
das Steak dahs shtayhk	steak
der Tafelspitz dehr <u>tah</u>·fehl·shpeets	Viennese-style boiled beef
der Truthahn dehr <u>troot</u>·hahn	turkey

rare	**roh** roh
medium	**medium** <u>meh</u>·dee·uhm
well-done	**durchgebraten** <u>doorkh</u>·geh·brah·tuhn

I can't have…	**Ich vertrage *kein/keine* …** eekh fehr·<u>trah</u>·guh *kien/<u>kien</u>·uh* …

▶ For when to use **kein** or **keine**, see page 164.

das Wiener Schnitzel dahs <u>viee</u>·nehr <u>shniht</u>·tzehl   veal cutlet

die Wurst dee voorst   sausage

die Zunge dee <u>tsoong</u>·uh   tongue

Vegetables and Staples

die Artischocke dee ahr·tee·<u>shoh</u>·kuh   artichoke

die Aubergine dee <u>ow</u>·behr·gee·neh   eggplant [aubergine]

die Avocado dee ah·voh·<u>kah</u>·doh   avocado

die Bohnen dee <u>boh</u>·nuhn   beans

die grünen Bohnen dee <u>grew</u>·nuhn <u>boh</u>·nuhn   green beans

der Blumenkohl dehr <u>bloo</u>·muhn·kohl   cauliflower

der Brokkoli dehr <u>broh</u>·koh·lee   broccoli

die Erbse dee <u>ehrb</u>·zuh   pea

das gemischte Gemüse dahs geh·<u>meesh</u>·tuh geh·<u>mew</u>·zuh   mixed vegetables

das Gemüse dahs geh·<u>mew</u>·zuh   vegetable

die Gurke dee <u>goor</u>·kuh   cucumber

die Kartoffel dee kahr·<u>toh</u>·fuhl   potato

der Kartoffelbrei dehr kahr·<u>toh</u>·fehl·brie   mashed potato

der Knoblauch dehr <u>knoh</u>·blowkh   garlic

der Kohl dehr kohl   cabbage

I'd like…	**Ich möchte gern …** eekh <u>merkh</u>·tuh gehrn …
More…, please.	**Mehr …, bitte.** mehr … <u>biht</u>·tuh
With/Without…	**Mit/Ohne …** miht/<u>oh</u>·nuh …

der Krautsalat dehr <u>krowt</u>·sah·laht	coleslaw
der Mais dehr mies	corn
der Maiskolben dehr <u>mies</u>·kohl·behn	corn on the cob
die Möhre dee <u>mer</u>·ruh	carrot
die Olive dee oh·<u>lee</u>·vuh	olive
der *rote/grüne* Paprika dehr <u>*roh*</u>·*teh/* <u>*grew*</u>·*neh* pah·<u>pree</u>·kuh	*red/green* pepper
die Pasta dee <u>pah</u>·stah	pasta
die Pellkartoffeln dee <u>pehl</u>·kahr·toh·fehl·ehn	boiled, unpeeled potatoes
der Pilz dehr pihlts	mushroom
der Reis dehr ries	rice
der Rettich dehr <u>reh</u>·teekh	radish
das Roggenbrot dahs <u>roh</u>·gehn·broht	rye bread
der Salat dehr sah·<u>laht</u>	lettuce
der Spargel dehr <u>shpahr</u>·gehl	asparagus
der Spinat dehr shpee·<u>naht</u>	spinach
die Tomate dee toh·<u>mah</u>·teh	tomato
die Zucchini dee tsoo·<u>khee</u>·nee	zucchini [courgette]
die Zwiebel dee <u>tsvee</u>·buhl	onion

Fruit

die Ananas dee <u>ah</u>·nah·nahs	pineapple
der Apfel dehr <u>ahp</u>·fuhl	apple

I can't have…	**Ich vertrage *kein/keine* …** eekh fehr·<u>trah</u>·guh *kien/<u>kien</u>·uh* …

▶ For when to use **kein** or **keine**, see page 164.

die Apfelsine dee ah·pfehl·<u>zee</u>·nuh	orange
die Banane dee bah·<u>nah</u>·nuh	banana
die Birne dee <u>beer</u>·nuh	pear
die Blaubeere dee <u>blow</u>·beh·ruh	blueberry
die Erdbeere dee <u>ehrd</u>·beh·ruh	strawberry
die Himbeere dee <u>hihm</u>·beh·ruh	raspberry
die Kirsche dee <u>keer</u>·shuh	cherry
die Limette dee lee·<u>meh</u>·tuh	lime
die Melone dee meh·<u>loh</u>·nuh	melon
das Obst dahs ohpst	fruit
die Pampelmuse dee <u>pahm</u>·pehl·moo·zuh	grapefruit
der Pfirsich dehr <u>pfeer</u>·zeekh	peach
die Pflaume dee <u>pflow</u>·muh	plum
die *rote/schwarze* Johannisbeere dee <u>roh</u>·tuh/<u>shvahr</u>·tsuh yoh·<u>hah</u>·nihs·beh·ruh	*red/black* currant
die Weintraube dee <u>vien</u>·trow·buh	grape
die Zitrone dee tsee·<u>troh</u>·nuh	lemon

Cheese

der Appenzeller dehr <u>ah</u>·pehn·tseh·lehr	hard cheese from Switzerland
der Blauschimmelkäse dehr <u>blow</u>·shihm·mehl·kay·zuh	blue cheese

I'd like…	**Ich möchte gern …** eekh <u>merkh</u>·tuh gehrn …
More…, please.	**Mehr .., bitte.** mehr … <u>biht</u>·tuh
With/Without…	**Mit/Ohne …** miht/<u>oh</u>·nuh …

der Emmentaler dehr <u>ehm</u>·mehn·tah·lehr — mild Swiss cheese

der Frischkäse dehr <u>freesh</u>·kay·zuh — cream cheese

der Handkäse dehr <u>hahnt</u>·kay·zuh — sharp, soft cheese

die Käseplatte dee <u>kay</u>·zuh·plah·tuh — cheese platter

der Schafskäse dehr <u>shahf</u>·kay·zuh — feta cheese

der Tilsiter dehr <u>teel</u>·seet·ehr — semi-soft Austrian cheese

der Ziegenkäse dehr <u>tsee</u>·guhn·kay·zuh — goat cheese

Dessert

der Apfelkuchen dehr <u>ah</u>·pfuhl·kookh·uhn — apple pie or tart

das Eis dahs ies — ice cream

der Käsekuchen dehr <u>kay</u>·zuh·kookh·uhn — cheesecake

der Krapfen dehr <u>krah</u>·pfehn — fritter

die Makrone dee mah·<u>kroh</u>·nuh — macaroon

das Marzipan dahs <u>mahr</u>·tsee·pahn — marzipan

der Obstsalat dehr <u>ohpst</u>·sah·laht — fruit salad

die Rote Grütze dee <u>roh</u>·tuh <u>grewt</u>·zuh — berry pudding

die Schwarzwälder Kirschtorte dee <u>schvahrts</u>·vahl·dehr <u>keersh</u>·tohr·tuh — Black Forest chocolate cake with cherries

die Torte dee <u>tohr</u>·tuh — cake

I can't have… **Ich vertrage *kein/keine* …** eekh fehr·<u>trah</u>·guh *kien/<u>kien</u>·uh* …

▶For when to use **kein** or **keine**, see page 164.

Drinks

Essential

The *wine list/drink menu*, please.	**Die *Weinkarte/Getränkekarte*, bitte.** dee *vien·kahr·tuh/geh·trehnk·uh·kahr·tuh* biht·tuh
What do you recommend?	**Was empfehlen Sie?** vahs ehm·pfeh·luhn zee
I'd like a *bottle/ glass* of *red/ white* wine.	**Ich möchte gern *eine Flasche/ein Glas Rotwein/Weißwein.*** eekh merkh·tuh gehrn *ien·uh flah·shuh/ien* glahs *roht·vien/vies·vien*
The house wine, please.	**Den Hauswein, bitte.** dehn hows·vien biht·tuh
Another *bottle/glass*, please.	**Noch *eine Flasche/ein Glas*, bitte.** nohkh *ien·uh flah·shuh/ien* glahs biht·tuh
I'd like a local beer.	**Ich möchte gern ein Bier aus der Region.** eekh merkh·tuh gehrn ien beer ows dehr rehg·yohn
Can I buy you a drink?	**Darf ich Ihnen einen ausgeben?** dahrf eekh eehn·uhn ows·geh·buhn
Cheers!	**Prost!** prohst
A *coffee/tea*, please.	**Einen *Kaffee/Tee*, bitte.** ien·uhn *kah·feh/tee* biht·tuh
Black.	**Schwarz.** shvahrts
With…	**Mit …** miht …
– milk	**– Milch** mihlkh
– sugar	**– Zucker** tsoo·kehr
– artificial sweetener	**– Süßstoff** zews·shtohf
…, please.	**…, bitte.** … biht·tuh
– A juice	**– Einen Saft** ien·uhn zahft

– A soda   **– Eine Cola** <u>ien</u>·uh <u>koh</u>·lah

– A *still/sparkling* water   **– Ein *stilles Wasser/Wasser mit Kohlensäure*** ien <u>shtihl</u>·uhs <u>vah</u>·sehr/<u>vah</u>·sehr miht <u>kohl</u>·ehn·zoy·ruh

Non-alcoholic Drinks

die Cola dee <u>koh</u>·lah	soda
der Kaffee dehr kah·<u>feh</u>	coffee
der Kakao dehr kah·<u>kah</u>·ow	hot chocolate
die Milch dee mihlkh	milk
der Saft dehr zahft	juice
der (Eis-)Tee dehr (ies) tee	(iced) tea
das *stille Wasser/Wasser mit Kohlensäure* dahs <u>shtihl</u>·uh <u>vah</u>·sehr/<u>vah</u>·sehr miht <u>kohl</u>·ehn·zoy·ruh	*still/sparkling* water

i **Kaffee** (coffee) is popular in Germany and a fresh cup can be found at a **Café** or **Kaffeehaus**. **Kräutertee** (herbal tea) is another common beverage, and pharmacies, supermarkets and health-food stores carry a variety of teas.

You May Hear...

Möchten Sie etwas trinken? <u>merkh</u>·tuhn zee <u>eht</u>·vahs <u>trihn</u>·kuhn   Can I get you a drink?

Mit Milch oder Zucker? miht mihlkh <u>oh</u>·dehr <u>tsoo</u>·kchr   With milk or sugar?

Stilles Wasser oder mit Kohlensäure? <u>shtihl</u>·uhs <u>vah</u>·sehr <u>oh</u>·dehr miht <u>koh</u>·lehn·zoy·ruh   Sparkling or still water?

Aperitifs, Cocktails and Liqueurs

der Gin dehr djihn	gin
der Rum dehr room	rum
der Scotch dehr skohch	scotch
der Tequila dehr teh-_kee_-lah	tequila
der Weinbrand dehr _vien_-brahnt	brandy
der Whisky dehr _vees_-kee	whisky
der Wodka dehr _voht_-kah	vodka

Beer

das Flaschenbier dahs _flah_-shuhn-beer	bottled beer
das Bier vom Fass dahs beer fohm fahs	draft beer
das _Helle/Pilsner_ dahs _heh_-luh/_pihls_-nehr	_lager/pilsner_
die Halbe dee _hahlb_-uh	pint
das ... Bier dahs ... beer	...beer
– **dunkle/helle** _doon_-kluh/_heh_-luh	– dark/light
– **regionale/importierte** reh-gyoh-_nah_-luh/ eem-pohr-_teer_-tuh	– local/imported
– **alkoholfreie** ahl-koh-hohl-_frie_-uh	– non-alcoholic

i There are more than 1,000 breweries in Germany, producing more than 5,000 different brands of beer.

Styles include: **Altbier** (high hops content, similar to British ale), **Bockbier** (high malt content), **Hefeweizen** (pale, made from wheat), **Kölsch** (lager, brewed in Cologne), **Malzbier** (dark and sweet) and **Pilsener** (pale and strong). Popular German brands include: **Augustiner**™, **Beck's**™, **Jever**™, **Löwenbräu**™ and **Spaten**™.

Wine

der Champagner dehr shahm·<u>pahn</u>·yehr	champagne
der Wein dehr vien	wine
der Dessertwein dehr deh·<u>sehrt</u>·vien	dessert wine
der *Hauswein/Tischwein* dehr <u>hows</u>·vien/<u>tihsh</u>·vien	*house/table* wine
der *Rotwein/Weißwein* dehr <u>roht</u>·vien/<u>vies</u>·vien	*red/white* wine
der *trockene/liebliche* Wein dehr <u>troh</u>·keh·neh/<u>lee</u>·blee·kheh vien	*dry/sweet wine*
der Schaumwein dehr <u>showm</u>·vien	sparkling wine

Menu Reader

der Aal dehr ahl — eel

die Ananas dee ahn·ah·nahs — pineapple

der Aperitif dehr ah·pehr·ee·teef — aperitif

der Apfel dehr ahp·fehl — apple

die Apfelsine dee ah·pfuhl·zee·nuh — orange

der Apfelwein dehr ah·pfuhl·vien — cider (alcoholic)

die Aprikose dee ah·pree·koh·zuh — apricot

die Artischocke dee ahr·tee·shoh·kuh — artichoke

die Aubergine dee ow·behr·gee·nuh — eggplant [aubergine]

der Aufschnitt dehr owf·shniht — cold cuts [charcuterie]

die Auster dee ows·tuhr — oyster

die Avocado dee ah·voh·kah·doh — avocado

die Backpflaume dee bahk·pflow·muh — prune

der Bacon dehr bah·kohn — bacon

die Banane dee bah·<u>nah</u>·nuh	banana
der Barsch dehr bahrsh	bass
das Basilikum dahs bah·<u>zee</u>·lee·koom	basil
das Bier dahs beer	beer
die Birne dee <u>beer</u>·nuh	pear
die Blaubeere dee <u>blow</u>·beh·ruh	blueberry
der Blauschimmelkäse dehr <u>blow</u>·shihm·mehl·kay·zuh	blue cheese
der Blumenkohl dehr <u>bloo</u>·muhn·kohl	cauliflower
die Blutwurst dee <u>bloot</u>·voorst	blood sausage
die Bohne dee <u>boh</u>·nuh	bean
die Bouillon dee boo·<u>yohn</u>	broth
der Branntwein dehr <u>brahnt</u>·vien	brandy
der Braten dehr <u>brah</u>·tuhn	roast
die Brombeere dee <u>brohm</u>·beh·ruh	blackberry
das Brot dahs broht	bread
das Brötchen dahs <u>brert</u>·khehn	roll
die Brunnenkresse dee <u>broo</u>·nuhn·kreh·zuh	watercress
die (Hühnchen-) Brust dee (<u>hewn</u>·khehn-) broost	breast (of chicken)
die Butter dee <u>boo</u>·tehr	butter
die Buttermilch dee <u>boo</u>·tehr·mihlkh	buttermilk
die Cashewnuss dee keh·<u>shoo</u>·noos	cashew
der Chikorée dehr <u>chee</u>·koh·reh	chicory
die Chilischote dee <u>chee</u>·lee·shoh·tuh	chili pepper
die Cola dee <u>koh</u>·lah	soda
der Cracker dehr <u>kreh</u>·kehr	cracker

die Datteln dee <u>dah</u>·tuhln	dates
der Dessertwein dehr deh·<u>zehrt</u>·vien	dessert wine
der Dill dehr dihl	dill
der Donut dehr <u>doh</u>·nuht	doughnut
der Dorsch dehr dohrsh	cod
das Ei dahs ie	egg
das Eigelb dahs <u>ie</u>·gehlb	egg yolk
der Eierkuchen dehr <u>ier</u>·koo·khuhn	pancake
das Eis dahs ies	ice cream
der Eiswürfel dehr <u>ies</u>·vewr·fehl	ice (cube)
das Eiweiß dahs <u>ie</u>·vies	egg white
die Endivie dee ehn·<u>dee</u>·vee·uh	endive
die Ente dee <u>ehn</u>·tuh	duck
die Erbsen dee <u>ehrb</u>·zuhn	peas
die Erdbeere dee <u>ehrd</u>·beh·ruh	strawberry
die Erdnuss dee <u>ehrd</u>·noos	peanut
der Essig dehr <u>eh</u>·zeek	vinegar
das Estragon dahs <u>eh</u>·strah·gohn	tarragon
der Fasan dehr fah·<u>zahn</u>	pheasant
die Feige dee <u>fie</u>·guh	fig
der Fenchel dehr <u>fehn</u>·khehl	fennel
der Fisch dehr fihsh	fish
das Fleisch dahs fliesh	meat
die Fleischstücke dee <u>fliesh</u>·shtew·kuh	chopped meat
die Forelle dee foh·<u>reh</u>·luh	trout
die Gans dee gahns	goose
die Gänseleberpastete dee <u>gehn</u>·zehl·leh·behr·pah·steh·tuh	goose liver pâté

die Garnele dee gahr·neh·luh	shrimp
das Gebäck dahs guh·behk	pastry
das Geflügel dahs guh·flew·gehl	poultry
das Gemüse dahs geh·mew·zuh	vegetable
die Gewürze dee guh·vewr·tsuh	spices
die Gewürzgurke dee guh·vewrts·goor·kuh	pickle/gherkin
der Gin dehr djihn	gin
der Granatapfel dehr grah·naht·ahp·fehl	pomegranate
die grünen Bohnen dee grew·nuhn boh·nuhn	green beans
die Guave dee gwah·veh	guava
die Gurke dee goor·kuh	cucumber
die Hachse dee hahk·suh	shank
der Hamburger dehr hahm·boor·gehr	hamburger
der Hammel dehr hah·mehl	mutton
die Haselnuss dee hah·zuhl·noos	hazelnut
der Heilbutt dehr hiel·boot	halibut
die Henne dee heh·nuh	hen
der Hering dehr heh·reeng	herring
das Herz dahs hehrts	heart
die Himbeere dee heem·beh·ruh	raspberry
der Honig dehr hoh·neek	honey
der Hotdog dehr hoht·dohg	hot dog
das Hühnchen dahs hewn·khehn	chicken
der Hummer dehr hoo·mehr	lobster
der Hüttenkäse dehr hew·tuhn·kay·zuh	cottage cheese
der Imbiss dehr ihm·buhs	snack
der Ingwer dehr eeng·vehr	ginger

die Innereien dee ihn·eh·rie·uhn	organ meat [offal]
der Joghurt dehr yoh·goort	yogurt
der Kaffee dehr kah·feh	coffee
das Kalb dahs kahlb	veal
das Kaninchen dahs kah·neen·khehn	rabbit
die Kaper dee kah·pehr	caper
das Karamell dahs kah·rah·mehl	caramel
die Kartoffel dee kahr·toh·fehl	potato
die Kartoffelchips dee kahr·toh·fehl·cheeps	potato chips [crisps]
der Käse dehr kay·zuh	cheese
die Kastanie dee kah·stahn·yuh	chestnut
der Keks dehr keks	cookie [biscuit]
der Kerbel dehr kehr·behl	chervil
der Ketchup dehr keh·chuhp	ketchup
die Kichererbse dee kee·khehr·ehrb·zuh	chickpea
die Kirsche dee keer·shuh	cherry
die Kiwi dee kee·vee	kiwi
der Kloß dehr klohs	dumpling
der Knoblauch dehr knoh·blowkh	garlic
die Koblauchsauce dee knoh·blowkh·zow·suh	garlic sauce
der Kohl dehr kohl	cabbage
die Kokosnuss dee koh·kohs·noos	coconut
das Kompott dahs kohm·poht	stewed fruit
die Konfitüre dee kohn·fee·tew·ruh	jelly
der Koriander dehr koh·ree·ahn·dehr	cilantro [coriander]
die Kräuter dee kroyt·uhr	herbs

die Kraftbrühe dee <u>krahft</u>·brew·uh	consommé
der Krebs dehr krehbs	crab
das Krustentier dahs <u>kroos</u>·tehn·tyehr	shellfish
der Kuchen dehr <u>kookh</u>·uhn	pie
der Kümmel dehr <u>kew</u>·mehl	caraway
der Kürbis dehr <u>kewr</u>·bees	squash
die Kutteln dee <u>koo</u>·tehln	tripe
der Lachs dehr lahks	salmon
das Lamm dahs lahm	lamb
die Lauchzwiebel dee <u>lowkh</u>·svee·buhl	scallion [spring onion]
die Leber dee <u>leh</u>·buhr	liver
die Lende dee <u>lehn</u>·duh	loin
das Lendenfilet dahs lehn·dehn·<u>fee</u>·leh	sirloin
der Likör dehr lee·<u>ker</u>	liqueur
die Limette dee lee·<u>meh</u>·tuh	lime
die Limonade dee lee·moh·<u>nah</u>·duh	lemonade
die Linse dee <u>leen</u>·zuh	lentil
das Loorbeerblatt dahs <u>lohr</u>·behr·blaht	bay leaf
der Mais dehr mies	sweet corn
das Maismehl dahs <u>mies</u>·mehl	cornmeal
die Makkaroni dee mah·kah·<u>roh</u>·nee	macaroni
die Makrele dee mah·<u>krehl</u>·uh	mackerel
die Mandarine dee mahn·dah·<u>reen</u>·uh	tangerine
die Mandel dee <u>mahn</u>·duhl	almond
die Mango dee <u>mahn</u>·goh	mango
die Margarine dee mahr·guh·<u>ree</u>·nuh	margarine
die Marmelade dee mahr·muh·<u>lah</u>·duh	marmalade/jam

das Marzipan dahs mahr·tsee·pahn	marzipan
die Mayonnaise dee mah·yoh·nay·zuh	mayonnaise
die Meerbarbe dee mehr·bahr·buh	red mullet
die Meeresfrüchte dee meh·rehs·frewkh·tuh	seafood
die Melone dee meh·loh·nuh	melon
die Milch dee mihlkh	milk
das Milchmixgetränk dahs mihlkh·mihks·geh·traynk	milk shake
die Minze dee mihn·tsuh	mint
die Möhre dee mer·ruh	carrot
die Muschel dee moo·shehl	clam
der Muskat dehr moos·kaht	nutmeg
die Nelke dee nehl·kuh	clove
die Niere dee nee·ruh	kidney
die Nudel dee noo·dehl	noodle
der Nugat dehr noo·gaht	nougat
die Nüsse dee new·suh	nuts
das Obst dahs ohbst	fruit
der Ochse dehr ohkh·suh	ox
der Ochsenschwanz dehr ohk·sehn·shvahnts	oxtail
der Oktopus dehr ohk·toh·poos	octopus
die Olive dee oh·lee·veh	olive
das Olivenöl dahs oh·lee·vehn·erl	olive oil
das Omelett dahs ohm·leht	omelet
der Orangenlikör dehr oh·rahn·jehn·lee·ker	orange liqueur
das Oregano dahs oh·reh·gah·noh	oregano
die Pampelmuse dee pahm·puhl·moo·zuh	grapefruit

der Pansen dehr pahn·sehn	tripe
die Papaya dee pah·<u>pah</u>·yah	papaya
der Paprika dehr <u>pah</u>·pree·kuh	paprika
die Paprikaschote dee <u>pah</u>·pree·kah·shoh·tuh	pepper (vegetable)
die Pastinake dee pah·stee·<u>nahk</u>·uh	parsnip
die Pekannuss dee <u>peh</u>·kahn·noos	pecan
das Perlhuhn dahs <u>pehrl</u>·hoon	guinea fowl
die Petersilie dee peh·tehr·<u>see</u>·lee·uh	parsley
der Pfannkuchen dehr <u>pfahn</u>·koo·khuhn	pancake
der Pfeffer dehr <u>pfeh</u>·fehr	pepper (seasoning)
der Pfirsich dehr <u>pfeer</u>·zeekh	peach
die Pflaume dee <u>pflow</u>·muh	plum
der Pilz dehr pihlts	mushroom
die Pizza dee <u>pee</u>·tsah	pizza
die Pommes frites dee pohm freets	French fries
der Porree dehr <u>poh</u>·reh	leek
der Portwein dehr <u>pohrt</u>·vien	port
die Preiselbeere dee <u>prie</u>·zuhl·beh·ruh	cranberry
der Rahmkäse dehr <u>rahm</u>·kay·zuh	cream cheese
der Reis dehr ries	rice
der Rettich dehr <u>reh</u>·teekh	radish
der Rhabarber dehr rah·<u>bahr</u>·behr	rhubarb
der Rinderbraten dehr <u>reen</u>·dehr·brah·tuhn	roast beef
das Rindfleisch dahs <u>rihnt</u>·fliesh	beef
der Rosenkohl dehr <u>roh</u>·zuhn·kohl	Brussels sprouts
die Rosine dee roh·<u>zee</u>·nuh	raisin
der Rosmarin dehr <u>rohs</u>·mah·reen	rosemary

die rote Johannisbeere dee <u>roh</u>·tuh yoh·<u>hah</u>·nihs·beh·ruh — red currant

der Rotkohl dehr <u>roht</u>·kohl — red cabbage

die Rübe dee <u>rew</u>·beh — beet/turnip

der Rum dehr room — rum

der Safran dehr <u>zahf</u>·rahn — saffron

der Saft dehr zahft — juice

die Sahne dee <u>zah</u>·nuh — cream

die Salami dee zah·<u>lah</u>·mee — salami

der Salat dehr sah·<u>laht</u> — lettuce/salad

der Salbei dehr <u>zahl</u>·bie — sage

das Salz dahs zahlts — salt

das Sandwich dahs <u>sahnd</u>·weetsh — sandwich

die Sardelle dee sahr·<u>dehl</u>·uh — anchovy

die Sardine dee zahr·<u>dee</u>·nuh — sardine

die Sauce dee <u>zows</u>·uh — sauce

die Sauerkirsche dee <u>zow</u>·ehr·keer·shuh — sour cherry

die saure Sahne dee <u>zow</u>·ruh <u>zah</u>·nuh — sour cream

die Schalotte dee shah·<u>loh</u>·tuh — shallot

die scharfe Pfeffersauce dee <u>shahr</u>·fuh <u>pfeh</u>·fehr·zow·suh — hot pepper sauce

das Schaumgebäck dahs <u>showm</u>·guh·behk — meringue

der Schellfisch dehr <u>shehl</u>·fihsh — haddock

der Schinken dehr <u>sheen</u>·kuhn — ham

die Schlagsahne dee <u>shlahg</u>·zah·nuh — whipped cream

die Schnecke dee <u>shnehkh</u>·uh — snail

der Schnittlauch dehr <u>shniht</u>·lowkh — chives

das Schnitzel dahs <u>shniht</u>·tzuhl	chop
die Schokolade dee shoh·koh·<u>lah</u>·duh	chocolate
die Schulter dee <u>shool</u>·tehr	shoulder
die schwarze Johannisbeere dee <u>shvahr</u>·tsuh yoh·<u>hah</u>·nees·beh·ruh	black currant
das Schweinefleisch dahs <u>shvien</u>·uh·fliesh	pork
der Schwertfisch dehr <u>shvehrt</u>·fihsh	swordfish
der Scotch dehr skohtsh	scotch
der Seebarsch dehr <u>zeh</u>·bahrsh	sea bass
der Seehecht dehr <u>zeh</u>·hehkht	hake
der Seeteufel dehr <u>zeh</u>·toy·fuhl	monkfish
die Seezunge dee <u>zeh</u>·tsoong·uh	sole
der Sellerie dehr <u>zeh</u>·luh·ree	celery
der Senf dehr zehnf	mustard
der Sherry dehr <u>shehr</u>·ee	sherry
der Sirup dehr <u>zew</u>·roop	syrup
das Soda-Wasser dahs <u>soh</u>·dah-<u>vah</u>·sehr	soda water
die Sojabohne dee <u>zoh</u>·yah·boh·nuh	soybean [soya bean]
die Sojamilch dee <u>zoh</u>·yah·mihlkh	soymilk [soya milk]
die Sojasauce dee <u>zoh</u>·yah·zow·suh	soy sauce
die Sojasprossen dee <u>soh</u>·jah·shproh·suhn	bean sprouts
die Spaghetti dee shpah·<u>geh</u>·tee	spaghetti
das Spanferkel dahs <u>shpahn</u>·fehr·kehl	crunchy roasted suckling pig
der Spargel dehr <u>shpahr</u>·gehl	asparagus
der Spinat dehr shpee·<u>naht</u>	spinach
die Spirituosen dee shpee·ree·<u>twoh</u>·zuhn	spirits

die Stachelbeere dee <u>shtah</u>·khehl·beh·ruh	gooseberry
das Steak dahs stehk	steak
die Suppe dee <u>zoo</u>·puh	soup
die Süßigkeiten dee <u>zew</u>·seekh·kie·tuhn	candy [sweets]
die Süßkartoffel dee <u>zews</u>·kahr·toh·fuhl	sweet potato
die süßsaure Sauce dee <u>zews</u>·zow·ruh <u>zow</u>·suh	sweet and sour sauce
der Süßstoff dehr <u>zews</u>·shtohf	sweetener
der Tee dehr teh	tea
der Thunfisch dehr <u>toon</u>·fihsh	tuna
der Thymian dehr <u>tew</u>·mee·ahn	thyme
der Tintenfisch dehr <u>teen</u>·tuhn·fihsh	squid
der Toast dehr tohst	toast
das Tofu dahs <u>toh</u>·foo	tofu
die Tomate dee <u>toh</u>·mah·tuh	tomato
das Tonic dahs <u>toh</u>·neek	tonic water
die Trüffel dee <u>trew</u>·fuhl	truffles
der Truthahn dehr <u>troot</u>·hahn	turkey
die Vanille dee vah·<u>nee</u>·luh	vanilla
die Wachtel dee <u>vahkh</u>·tehl	quail
die Waffel dee <u>vah</u>·fuhl	waffle
die Walnuss dee <u>vahl</u>·noos	walnut
das Wasser dahs <u>vah</u>·sehr	water
die Wassermelone dee <u>vah</u>·sehr·meh·loh·nuh	watermelon
der Wein dehr vien	wine
die Weintrauben dee <u>vien</u>·trow·buhn	grapes
der Weizen dehr <u>vie</u>·tsuhn	wheat

der Wermut dehr <u>vehr</u>·moot — vermouth

der Whisky dehr <u>vees</u>·kee — whisky

das Wild dahs vihlt — game/venison

der Wodka dehr <u>vohd</u>·kah — vodka

die Wurst dee voorst — sausage

der Zackenbarsch dehr <u>tsah</u>·kehn·bahrsh — sea perch

das Zicklein dahs <u>tsihk</u>·lien — kid (young goat)

die Ziege dee <u>tsee</u>·guh — goat

der Ziegenkäse dehr <u>tsee</u>·guhn·kay·zuh — goat cheese

der Zimt dehr tsihmt — cinnamon

die Zitrone dee tsee·<u>troh</u>·nuh — lemon

die Zucchini dee tsoo·<u>kee</u>·nee — zucchini [courgette]

der Zucker dehr <u>tsoo</u>·kehr — sugar

die Zunge dee <u>tsoong</u>·uh — tongue

die Zwiebel dee <u>tsvee</u>·buhl — onion

▼ People

Essential

Hello!	**Hallo!** hah·<u>loh</u>
How are you?	**Wie geht es Ihnen?** vee geht ehs <u>eehn</u>·uhn
Fine, thanks.	**Gut, danke.** goot <u>dahn</u>·kuh
Excuse me!	**Entschuldigung!** ehnt·<u>shool</u>·dee·goong
Do you speak English?	**Sprechen Sie Englisch?** <u>shpreh</u>·khuhn zee <u>ehn</u>·gleesh
What's your name?	**Wie heißen Sie?** vee <u>hie</u>·suhn zee
My name is…	**Mein Name ist …** mien <u>nahm</u>·uh ihst …
Nice to meet you.	**Schön, Sie kennenzulernen.** shern zee <u>keh</u>·nehn·tsoo·lehr·nehn
Where are you from?	**Woher kommen Sie?** <u>voh</u>·hehr <u>koh</u>·muhn zee
I'm from the *U.S./U.K.*	**Ich komme aus *den USA/Großbritannien.*** eekh <u>koh</u>·muh ows dehn <u>oo</u>·ehs·<u>ah</u>/ grohs·bree·<u>tah</u>·nee·ehn
What do you do?	**Was machen Sie beruflich?** vahs <u>mah</u>·khuhn zee beh·<u>roof</u>·likh
I work for…	**Ich arbeite für …** eekh <u>ahr</u>·bie·tuh fewr …
I'm a student.	**Ich bin Student.** eekh bihn shtoo·<u>dehnt</u>
I'm retired.	**Ich bin Rentner.** eekh been <u>rehnt</u>·nehr
Do you like…?	**Mögen Sie …?** <u>mer</u>·guhn zee …
Goodbye.	**Auf Wiedersehen.** owf <u>vee</u>·dehr·zehn
See you later.	**Bis bald.** bihs bahld

Communication Difficulties

Do you speak English? **Sprechen Sie Englisch?** <u>shpreh</u>·khehn zee ehn·gleesh

Does anyone here speak English? **Spricht hier jemand Englisch?** shpreekht heer <u>yeh</u>·mahnt <u>ehn</u>·gleesh

I don't speak (much) German. **Ich spreche kein (nicht viel) Deutsch.** eekh <u>shpreh</u>·khuh kien (neekht feel) doych

Can you speak more slowly, please? **Können Sie bitte langsamer sprechen?** <u>ker</u>·nuhn zee <u>biht</u>·tuh <u>lahng</u>·sahm·ehr <u>shpreh</u>·khuhn

Can you repeat that, please? **Können Sie das bitte wiederholen?** <u>ker</u>·nuhn zee dahs <u>biht</u>·tuh vee·dehr·<u>hoh</u>·luhn

Excuse me? **Wie bitte?** vee <u>biht</u>·tuh

What was that? **Was haben Sie gesagt?** vahs <u>hah</u>·buhn zee guh·<u>zahgt</u>

Can you spell it?	**Können Sie das buchstabieren?** <u>ker</u>·nuhn zee dahs book·shtah·<u>bee</u>·ruhn
Write it down, please.	**Bitte schreiben Sie es auf.** <u>biht</u>·tuh <u>shrie</u>·buhn zee ehs owf
Can you translate this into English for me?	**Können Sie das für mich ins Englische übersetzen?** <u>ker</u>·nuhn zee dahs fewr meekh ihns <u>ehn</u>·glee·shuh ew·behr·<u>zeh</u>·tsuhn
What does... mean?	**Was bedeutet ...?** vahs beh·<u>doyt</u>·eht ...
I understand.	**Ich verstehe.** eekh fehr·<u>shteh</u>·uh
I don't understand.	**Ich verstehe nicht.** eekh fehr·<u>shteh</u>·uh neekht
Do you understand?	**Verstehen Sie?** fehr·<u>shteh</u>·uhn zee

You May Hear...

Ich spreche nur wenig Englisch.
eekh <u>shpreh</u>·khuh noor <u>veh</u>·neek <u>ehn</u>·gleesh

I only speak a little English.

Ich spreche kein Englisch.
eekh <u>shpreh</u>·khuh kien <u>ehn</u>·gleesh

I don't speak English.

Making Conversation

Hello!	**Hallo!** hah·<u>loh</u>
Good morning.	**Guten Morgen.** <u>goo</u>·tuhn <u>mohr</u>·guhn
Good afternoon.	**Guten Tag.** <u>goo</u>·tuhn tahk
Good evening.	**Guten Abend.** <u>goo</u>·tuhn <u>ah</u>·behnt
My name is...	**Mein Name ist ...** mien <u>nahm</u>·uh ihst ...
What's your name?	**Wie heißen Sie?** vee <u>hie</u>·sehn zee
I'd like to introduce you to...	**Ich möchte Sie gern ... vorstellen.** eekh <u>merkh</u>·tuh zee gehrn ... fohr·<u>shteh</u>·luhn

Pleased to meet you.	**Angenehm.** <u>ahn</u>·guh·nehm
How are you?	**Wie geht es Ihnen?** vee geht ehs <u>eehn</u>·uhn
Fine, thanks. And you?	**Gut, danke. Und Ihnen?** goot <u>dahn</u>·kuh oont <u>eehn</u>·uhn

 In Germany, it's polite to shake hands, both when you meet and say goodbye. Relatives and close friends may hug or kiss cheeks.

Travel Talk

I'm here on business.	**Ich bin geschäftlich hier.** eekh bihn guh·<u>shehft</u>·leekh heer
I'm here on vacation [holiday].	**Ich mache hier Urlaub.** eekh <u>mahkh</u>·uh heer <u>oor</u>·lowb
I'm studying here.	**Ich bin zum Studieren hier.** eekh bihn tsoom <u>shtoo</u>·dee·ruhn heer
I'm staying for...	**Ich bleibe ...** eekh <u>blie</u>·buh ...
I've been here...	**Ich bin seit ... hier.** eekh been ziet ... heer
– a day	**– einem Tag** <u>ien</u>·uhm tahk
– a week	**– einer Woche** <u>ien</u>·uhr <u>voh</u>·khuh
– a month	**– einem Monat** <u>ien</u>·uhm <u>moh</u>·naht

▶ For numbers, see page 167.

| Where are you from? | **Woher kommen Sie?** <u>voh</u>·hehr <u>koh</u>·muhn zee |
| I'm from... | **Ich komme aus ...** eekh <u>koh</u>·muh ows ... |

Relationships

| Who are you with? | **Mit wem sind Sie hier?** miht vehm zihnt zee heer |
| I'm here alone. | **Ich bin allein hier.** eekh bihn ah·<u>lien</u> heer |

I'm with…	**Ich bin mit … hier.** eekh been miht … heer
– my husband/wife	**– meinem Mann/meiner Frau** <u>mie</u>·nuhm mahn/<u>mie</u>·nuhr frow
– my boyfriend/ girlfriend	**– meinem Freund/meiner Freundin** <u>mie</u>·nuhm froynt/<u>mie</u>·nuhr <u>froyn</u>·dihn
– my friend(s)	**– meinem Freund/meinen Freunden** <u>mie</u>·nuhm froynt/<u>mie</u>·nuhn <u>froyn</u>·duhn
– my colleague(s)	**– meinem Kollegen/meinen Kollegen** <u>mie</u>·nuhm <u>koh</u>·leh·guhn/<u>mie</u>·nuhn <u>koh</u>·leh·guhn
When's your birthday?	**Wann haben Sie Geburtstag?** vahn <u>hah</u>·buhn zee guh·<u>boorts</u>·tahk
How old are you?	**Wie alt sind Sie?** vee ahlt zihnt zee
I'm…	**Ich bin …** eekh bihn …

▶ For numbers, see page 167.

Are you married?	**Sind Sie verheiratet?** zihnt zee fehr·<u>hie</u>·rah·tuht
I'm…	**Ich bin …** eekh bihn …
– single/in a relationship	**– ledig/in einer Beziehung** <u>leh</u>·deek/ihn <u>ien</u>·uhr beh·tsee·oong
– engaged/married	**– verlobt/verheiratet** fehr·<u>lohbt</u>/fehr·<u>hie</u>·rah·tuht
– divorced/separated	**– geschieden/getrennt lebend** geh·<u>shee</u>·dehn/geh·<u>trehnt</u> <u>leh</u>·buhnd
– widowed	**– verwitwet** fehr·<u>viht</u>·veht
Do you have *children/ grandchildren*?	**Haben Sie *Kinder/Enkelkinder*?** <u>hah</u>·buhn zee *<u>kihn</u>·dehr/<u>ehn</u>·kehl·kihn·dehr*

Work and School

What do you do?	**Was machen Sie beruflich?** vahs <u>mah</u>·khuhn zee beh·<u>roof</u>·leekh
What are you studying?	**Was studieren Sie?** vahs shtoo·<u>dee</u>·ruhn zee

I'm studying German.	**Ich studiere Deutsch.** eekh shtoo·<u>dee</u>·ruh doych
I...	**Ich ...** eekh ...
– work *full-time/ part-time*	– **arbeite *Vollzeit/Teilzeit*** <u>ahr</u>·bie·tuh *<u>fohl</u>·tsiet/<u>tiel</u>·tsiet*
– do freelance work	– **bin Freiberufler** bihn <u>frie</u>·beh·roo·flehr
– am a consultant	– **bin Berater** bihn beh·<u>rah</u>·tehr
– am unemployed	– **bin arbeitslos** bihn <u>ahr</u>·biets·lohs
– work at home	– **arbeite zu Hause** <u>ahr</u>·bie·tuh tsoo <u>how</u>·zuh
Who do you work for?	**Für wen arbeiten Sie?** fewr vehn <u>ahr</u>·bie·tuhn zee
I work for...	**Ich arbeite für ...** eekh <u>ahr</u>·bie·tuh fewr ...
Here's my business card.	**Hier ist meine Visitenkarte.** heer ihst <u>mie</u>·nuh vih·<u>zee</u>·tuhn·kahr·tuh

▶ For business travel, see page 139.

Weather

What's the forecast?	**Wie ist die Wettervorhersage?** vee ihst dee <u>veh</u>·tehr·fohr·hehr·zahg·uh
What *beautiful/terrible* weather!	**Was für ein *schönes/schlechtes* Wetter!** vahs fewr ien *<u>sher</u>·nuhs/<u>shlehkht</u>·uhs* <u>veh</u>·tehr
It's...	**Es ist ...** ehs ihst ...
cool/warm	**kühl/warm** kewl/vahrm
cold/hot	**kalt/heiß** kahlt/hies
rainy/sunny	**regnerisch/sonnig** <u>rehg</u>·nuh·reesh/<u>zoh</u>·neek
There is *snow/ice*	**Es gibt *Schnee/Eis*.** ehs gihbt shneh/ies
Do I need *a jacket/ an umbrella*?	**Brauche ich *eine Jacke/einen Regenschirm*?** <u>brow</u>·khuh eekh *<u>ien</u>·uh <u>yah</u>·kuh/<u>ien</u>·uhn <u>reh</u>·guhn·sheerm*

▶ For temperature, see page 174.

Essential

Would you like to go out for a *drink/dinner*?	**Möchten Sie mit mir *auf einen Drink/zum Essen* gehen?** merkh·tuhn zee miht meer *owf ien·uhn treenk/tsoom eh·suhn* geh·uhn
What are your plans for *tonight/tomorrow*?	**Was haben Sie *heute Abend/morgen* vor?** vahs hah·buhn zee *hoy·tuh ah·buhnt/mohr·guhn* fohr
Can I have your number?	**Kann ich Ihre Telefonnummer haben?** kahn eekh ee·ruh teh·leh·fohn·noo·mehr hah·buhn
Can I join you?	**Kann ich mitkommen?** kahn eekh miht·koh·muhn
Can I get you a drink?	**Darf ich Ihnen einen Drink ausgeben?** dahrf eekh eehn·uhn ien·uhn treenk ows·geh·buhn
I *like/love* you.	**Ich *mag/liebe* dich.** eekh *mahk/lee·buh* deekh

Making Plans

Would you like to go out for coffee?	**Möchten Sie mit mir Kaffee trinken gehen?** mehrkh·tuhn zee miht meer ien·uhn kah·feh trihnk·uhn geh·uhn
What are your plans for… ?	**Was haben Sie … vor?** vahs hah·buhn zee … fohr
– today	**– heute** hoy·tuh
– tonight	**– heute Abend** hoy·tuh ah·buhnt
– tomorrow	**– morgen** mohr·guhn
– this weekend	**– dieses Wochenende** dee·zuhs voh·khuhn·ehn·duh
Where would you like to go?	**Wohin möchten Sie gern gehen?** voh·hihn merkh·tuhn zee gehrn geh·uhn
I'd like to go…	**Ich möchte gern … gehen.** eekh merkh·tuh gehrn … geh·uhn

| Do you like…? | **Mögen Sie …?** <u>mer</u>·guhn zee … |
| Can I have your *number/e-mail*? | **Kann ich Ihre *Telefonnummer/E-Mail* haben?** kahn eekh <u>ee</u>·ruh *teh·leh·<u>fohn</u>·noo·mehr/<u>ee</u>·mehl* <u>hah</u>·buhn |

▶ For e-mail and phone, see page 49.

Pick-up [Chat-up] Lines

Can I join you?	**Kann ich mitkommen?** kahn eekh <u>miht</u>·koh·muhn
You're very attractive.	**Sie sind sehr attraktiv.** zee zihnt zehr aht·rahk·<u>teef</u>
Let's go somewhere quieter.	**Lassen Sie uns an einen ruhigeren Ort gehen.** <u>lah</u>·suhn zee oons ahn <u>ien</u>·uhn <u>roo</u>·ee·geh·ruhn ohrt <u>geh</u>·uhn

Accepting and Rejecting

| I'd love to. | **Gerne.** <u>gehr</u>·nuh |
| Where should we meet? | **Wo wollen wir uns treffen?** voh <u>voh</u>·luhn veer oons <u>treh</u>·fuhn |

I'll meet you at *the bar/your hotel*.	**Ich treffe Sie an *der Bar/Ihrem Hotel*.** eekh <u>treh</u>·fuh zee ahn *dehr bahr/<u>ee</u>·ruhm hoh·<u>tehl</u>*
I'll come by at…	**Ich komme um … vorbei.** eekh <u>koh</u>·muh oom … fohr·<u>bie</u>

▶For time, see page 169.

What is your address?	**Wie ist Ihre Adresse?** vee ihsht <u>ee</u>·ruh ah·<u>drehs</u>·uh
I'm busy.	**Ich bin beschäftigt.** eekh been beh·<u>shehf</u>·teekt
I'm not interested.	**Ich habe kein Interesse.** eekh <u>hah</u>·buh kien ihn·teh·<u>reh</u>·suh
Leave me alone.	**Lassen Sie mich in Ruhe.** <u>lah</u>·sehn zee meekh ihn <u>roo</u>·uh
Stop bothering me!	**Hören Sie auf, mich zu belästigen!** her·<u>ruhn</u> zee owf meekh tsoo buh·<u>lay</u>·steeg·uhn

Getting Physical

Can I *hug/kiss* you?	**Kann ich dich *umarmen/küssen*?** kahn eekh deekh *<u>oom</u>·ahr·muhn/<u>kew</u>·zuhn*
Yes.	**Ja.** yah
No.	**Nein.** nien
Stop!	**Stopp!** shtohp
I *like/love* you.	**Ich *mag/liebe* dich.** eekh *mahk/<u>lee</u>·buh* deekh

Sexual Preferences

Are you gay?	**Bist du schwul?** beesht doo shvool
I'm…	**Ich bin …** eekh been …
– heterosexual	**– heterosexuell** heh·tuh·roh·<u>sehks</u>·oo·ehl
– homosexual	**– homosexuell** hoh·moh·<u>sehks</u>·oo·ehl
– bisexual	**– bisexuell** bee·<u>sehks</u>·oo·ehl
Do you like *men/women*?	**Magst du *Männer/Frauen*?** mahgst doo *<u>meh</u>·nehr/<u>frow</u>·uhn*

▼ Fun

Sightseeing

Essential

Where's the tourist information office?	**Wo ist das Touristeninformationsbüro?** voh ihst dahs too·<u>ree</u>·stuhn·een·fohr·mah·syohns·bew·roh
What are the main attractions?	**Was sind die wichtigsten Sehenswürdigkeiten?** vahs zihnt dee <u>veekh</u>·teeg·stuhn <u>zeh</u>·uhns·vewr·deekh·kie·luhn
Do you have tours in English?	**Haben Sie Führungen in Englisch?** <u>hah</u>·buhn zee <u>few</u>·roong·uhn een <u>ehn</u>·gleesh
Can I have a *map/ guide*?	**Kann ich einen *Stadtplan/Reiseführer* haben?** kahn eekh <u>ien</u>·uhn <u>shtaht</u>·plahn/ rie·seh·<u>fewhr</u>·ehr <u>hah</u>·buhn

Tourist Information Office

Do you have information on...?	**Haben Sie Informationen über ...?** <u>hah</u>·buhn zee <u>ihn</u>·fohr·mah·syoh·nuhn <u>ew</u>·buhr ...
Can you recommend...?	**Können Sie ... empfehlen?** <u>ker</u>·nuhn zee ... ehm·<u>pfeh</u>·luhn
– a bus tour	**– eine Busreise** <u>ien</u>·uh <u>boos</u>·rie·zuh
– an excursion to...	**– einen Ausflug nach ...** <u>ien</u>·uhn <u>ows</u>·flook nahkh ...
– a sightseeing tour	**– eine Stadtrundfahrt** <u>ien</u>·uh <u>shtaht</u>·roond·fahrt

Tourist information offices are located throughout Germany. Look for ⓘ or ask your hotel concierge where the nearest office is located. Tourist information offices can recommend destinations, attractions, local events and festivals, and help you find hotels, tours, transportation and other services. Visit the **Deutsche Zentrale für Tourismus**, **DZT** (German center for tourism), website for more information.

Tours

I'd like to go on the tour to…
Ich möchte gern an der … Führung teilnehmen. *ish merkht·uh gehrn ahn dehr … fewhr·oong tiel·nehm·uh(n)*

When's the next tour?
Wann ist die nächste Führung? *vahn ihst dee nehkhst·uh fewhr·oong*

Are there tours in English?
Gibt es Führungen in Englisch? *gihpt ehs fewhr·oong·uhn ihn ehng·lihsh*

Is there an English *guide book/audio guide*?
Gibt es einen englischsprachigen *Reiseführer/Audio-Guide*? *gihpt ehs ien·uhn ehng·lihsh·shprahkh·ee·guhn riez·uh·fewhr·ehr/ ow·dee·oh·gied*

What time do we *leave/return*?
Wann *fahren wir ab/kommen wir wieder*? *vahn fahhr·uhn veer ap/kohm·uhn veer veed·ehr*

We'd like to see…
Wir möchten gern … sehen. *veer merkht·uhn gehrn … zeh·uhn*

Can we stop here…?
Können wir hier anhalten …? *ker·nuhn veer heer ahn·hahlt·uhn …*

– to take photos
– **um Fotos zu machen** *oom foht·ohs tsoo mahkh·uhn*

– for souvenirs
– **um Andenken zu kaufen** *oom ahn·dehnk·uhn tsoo kowf·uhn*

– for the restrooms [toilets]
– **um auf die Toilette zu gehen** *oom owf dee toy·leht·uh tsoo geh·uhn*

Is it handicapped [disabled]-accessible?
Ist es behindertengerecht? *ihst ehs beh·hihn·dehrt·uhn·geh·rehkht*

▶ For ticketing, see page 19.

Sights

Where's...?	**Wo ist ...?** voh ihst ...
– the battlefield	– **das Schlachtfeld** dahs shlahkht·fehlt
– the botanical garden	– **der botanische Garten** dehr boh·<u>tahn</u>·eesh·uh <u>gahr</u>·tuhn
– the castle	– **das Schloss** dahs shlohs
– the downtown area	– **das Stadtzentrum** dahs <u>shtadt</u>·tsehnt·room
– the fountain	– **der Brunnen** dehr <u>broon</u>·uhn
– the library	– **die Bücherei** dee bewkh·eh·<u>rie</u>
– the market	– **der Markt** dehr mahrkt
– the museum	– **das Museum** dahs moo·<u>zeh</u>·oom
– the old town	– **die Altstadt** dee <u>ahlt</u>·shtahdt
– the opera house	– **das Opernhaus** dahs <u>oh</u>·pehrn·hows
– the palace	– **der Palast** dehr pah·<u>lahst</u>
– the park	– **der Park** dehr pahrk
– the ruin	– **die Ruine** dee ro·<u>ee</u>·nuh
– the shopping area	– **das Einkaufszentrum** dahs <u>ien</u>·kowfs·tsehn·troom
– the theater	– **das Theater** dahs teh·<u>ah</u>·tehr
– the tower	– **der Turm** dehr toorm
– the town hall	– **das Rathaus** dahs <u>raht</u>·hows
– the town square	– **der Rathausplatz** dehr <u>raht</u>·hows·plats
Can you show me on the map?	**Können Sie mir das im Stadtplan zeigen?** <u>ker</u>·nuhn zee meer dahs ihm <u>shtadt</u>·plahn <u>tsie</u>·guhn

▶ For directions, see page 34.

Impressions

It's…	**Es ist …** ehs ihst …
– amazing	**– erstaunlich** ehr·<u>shtown</u>·leekh
– beautiful	**– wunderschön** <u>voond</u>·ehr·shern
– boring	**– langweilig** <u>lahng</u>·viel·eek
– interesting	**– interessant** ihn·teh·reh·<u>sahnt</u>
– magnificent	**– großartig** <u>groh</u>·sahr·teek
– romantic	**– romantisch** roh·<u>mahnt</u>·eesh
– strange	**– seltsam** <u>zehlt</u>·zahm
– stunning	**– umwerfend** <u>oom</u>·vehrf·uhnt
– terrible	**– schrecklich** <u>shrehk</u>·leekh
– ugly	**– hässlich** <u>hehs</u>·leekh
I (don't) like it.	**Es gefällt mir (nicht).** ehs guh·<u>fehlt</u> meer (neekht)

Religion

Where's…?	**Wo ist …?** voh ihst …
– the cathedral	**– die Kathedrale** dee kah·teh·<u>drah</u>l·uh
– the *Catholic/ Protestant* church	**– die *katholische/evangelische* Kirche** dee kah·<u>toh</u>·leesh·uh/eh·vahn·<u>gehl</u>·eesh·uh <u>keer</u>·khuh

– the mosque	**– die Moschee** dee moh·<u>sheh</u>
– the shrine	**– der Schrein** dehr shrien
– the synagogue	**– die Synagoge** dee zewn·uh·<u>goh</u>·guh
– the temple	**– der Tempel** dehr <u>tehm</u>·pehl
What time is *mass/ the service*?	**Wann ist *die Messe/der Gottesdienst*?** vahn ihst *dee <u>mehs</u>·suh/dehr <u>goht</u>·ehs·deenst*

Shopping

Essential

Where's the *market/ mall [shopping centre]*?	**Wo ist *der Markt/das Einkaufszentrum*?** voh ihst *dehr mahrkt/dahs ien·kowfs·tsehn·troom*
I'm just looking.	**Ich schaue mich nur um.** eekh <u>show</u>·uh meekh noor oom
Can you help me?	**Können Sie mir helfen?** <u>kern</u>·uhn zee meer <u>hehlf</u>·uhn
I'm being helped.	**Ich werde schon bedient.** eekh <u>vehrd</u>·uh shohn beh·<u>deent</u>
How much?	**Wie viel kostet das?** vee feel <u>kohs</u>·tuht dahs
That one, please.	**Dieses bitte.** <u>dee</u>·zuhs <u>biht</u>·tuh
That's all.	**Das ist alles.** dahs ihst <u>ahl</u>·uhs
Where can I pay?	**Wo kann ich bezahlen?** voh kahn eekh beh·<u>tsahl</u>·uhn
I'll pay *in cash/by credit card*.	**Ich zahle *bar/mit Kreditkarte*.** eekh tsahl·uh *bahr/miht kreh·<u>deet</u>·kahr·tuh*
A receipt, please.	**Eine Quittung, bitte.** <u>ien</u>·uh <u>kvih</u>·toong <u>biht</u>·tuh

Stores

Where's...?	**Wo ist ...?** voh ihst ...
– the antiques store	– **das Antiquitätengeschäft** dahs ahn·tee·kwee·<u>tay</u>·tuhn·guh·shehft
– the bakery	– **die Bäckerei** dee beh·keh·<u>rie</u>
– the bank	– **die Bank** dee bahnk
– the bookstore	– **der Buchladen** dehr <u>bookh</u>·lahd·uhn
– the clothing store	– **das Bekleidungsgeschäft** dahs buh·<u>klied</u>·oongs·guh·shehft
– the delicatessen	– **das Feinkostgeschäft** dahs <u>fien</u>·kohst·guh·shehft
– the department store	– **das Kaufhaus** dahs <u>kowf</u>·hows
– the gift shop	– **der Geschenkwarenladen** dehr guh·<u>shehnk</u>·vah·ruhn·lah·duhn
– the health food store	– **das Reformhaus** dahs reh·<u>fohrm</u>·hows
– the jeweler	– **das Schmuckgeschäft** dahs <u>shmook</u>·guh·shehft

– the liquor store [off-licence]	**das Spirituosengeschäft** dahs shpee·ree·<u>twoh</u>·zuhn·guh·shehft
– the market	**der Markt** dehr mahrkt
– the music store	**das Musikgeschäft** dahs moo·<u>zeek</u>·guh·shehft
– the pastry shop	**die Konditorei** dee kohn·dee·toh·<u>rie</u>
– the pharmacy [chemist]	**die Apotheke** dee ah·poh·<u>tehk</u>·uh
– the produce [grocery] store	**das Lebensmittelgeschäft** dahs <u>lehb</u>·uhns·miht·uhl·guh·shehft
– the shoe store	**das Schuhgeschäft** dahs <u>shooh</u>·guh·shehft
– the shopping mall [shopping centre]	**das Einkaufszentrum** dahs <u>ien</u>·kowfs·tsehn·troom
– the souvenir store	**der Andenkenladen** dehr <u>ahn</u>·dehnk·uhn·lah·duhn
– the supermarket	**der Supermarkt** dehr <u>zoo</u>·pehr·mahrkt
– the tobacco shop	**der Tabakladen** dehr tah·<u>bahk</u>·lahd·uhn
– the toy store	**das Spielzeuggeschäft** dahs <u>shpeel</u>·tsoyg·geh·shehft

Services

Can you recommend…?	**Können Sie … empfehlen?** <u>kern</u>·uhn zee … ehm·<u>pfeh</u>·luhn
– a barber	**einen Herrenfriseur** <u>ien</u>·uhn <u>hehr</u>·uhn·frih·zer
– a dry cleaner	**eine Reinigung** <u>ien</u>·uh <u>rien</u>·ee·goong
– a hairstylist	**einen Friseur** <u>ien</u>·uhn frih·<u>zer</u>
– a laundromat [launderette]	**einen Waschsalon** <u>ien</u>·uhn <u>vahsh</u>·zah·lohn
– a nail salon	**ein Nagelstudio** ien <u>nah</u>·gehl·shtood·yoh
– a spa	**ein Wellness-Center** ien <u>vehl</u>·nuhs·<u>sehn</u>·tehr
– a travel agency	**ein Reisebüro** ien <u>ric</u>·zuh·bew·roh

Can you...this?	**Können Sie das ...?** <u>kern</u>·uhn zee dahs ...
– alter	**– ändern** <u>ehn</u>·dehrn
– clean	**– reinigen** <u>rien</u>·ee·guhn
– fix [mend]	**– reparieren** reh·pah·<u>reer</u>·uhn
– press	**– bügeln** <u>bewg</u>·uhln
When will it be ready?	**Wann wird es fertig sein?** vahn veerd ehs <u>fehr</u>·teekh zien

Spa

I'd like...	**Ich möchte ...** eekh <u>merkht</u>·uh ...
– an *eyebrow/bikini* wax	**– eine Haarentfernung an *den Augenbrauen/der Bikinizone*** <u>ien</u>·uh <u>hahr</u>·ehnt·fehr·noong ahn *dehn <u>ow</u>·guhn·brow·uhn/dehr bee·<u>kee</u>·nee·tsoh·nuh*
– a facial	**– eine Gesichtsbehandlung** <u>ien</u>·uh guh·<u>zeekhts</u>·beh·hahnd·loong
– a *manicure/ pedicure*	**– eine *Maniküre/Pediküre*** <u>ien</u>·uh mah·nee·<u>kew</u>·ruh/peh·dee·<u>kew</u>·ruh
– a (sports) massage	**– eine (Sport-)Massage** <u>ien</u>·uh (shport-) mah·<u>sahdj</u>·uh
Do you do...?	**Machen Sie ...?** <u>mahk</u>·uhn zee ...
– acupuncture	**– Akupunktur** ah·koo·poonk·<u>toor</u>
– aromatherapy	**– Aromatherapie** ah·roh·mah·teh·<u>rah</u>·pee
– oxygen treatment	**– Sauerstoffbehandlung** <u>zow</u>·ehr·shtohf·beh·hahnd·loong
Do you have a sauna?	**Haben Sie eine Sauna?** <u>hah</u>·buhn zee <u>ien</u>·uh <u>zown</u>·ah

114

i Health resorts, day spas and hotel spas are popular destinations, and there are hundreds throughout Germany. Most spa towns have the word **Bad** in their names, for example: Bad Reichenhall, Europe's largest saline source, in Bavaria; Baden-Baden, considered the best and most fashionable; Wiesbaden, one of Germany's oldest cities and considered second best only to Baden-Baden; Bad Homburg, at the foot of Taunus Hills, once the summer retreat of Prussian kings; and Bad Nauheim, famous because both William Randolph Hearst and Elvis Presley were once guests experiencing the healing powers of the carbonic acid springs.

Tipping varies by spa; ask about the tipping policy when booking or upon arrival.

Hair Salon

I'd like…	**Ich möchte …** eekh <u>merkht</u>·uh …
– an appointment for *today/tomorrow*	– **einen Termin für *heute/morgen*** <u>ien</u>·uhn tehr·<u>meen</u> fewr <u>hoy</u>·tuh/<u>mohr</u>·guhn
– some *color/highlights*	– *die Haare/Strähnchen* **gefärbt bekommen** dee <u>hah</u>·ruh/<u>shtrehnkh</u>·uhn guh·<u>ferbt</u> buh·<u>kohm</u>·uhn
– my hair *styled/blow-dried*	– **mein Haar *stylen/fönen* lassen** mien hahr <u>shtew</u>·luhn/<u>fern</u>·uhn <u>lahs</u>·uhn
– a haircut	– **einen Haarschnitt** <u>ien</u>·uhn <u>hahr</u>·shniht
– a trim	– **die Haare nachschneiden lassen** dee <u>hahr</u>·uh <u>nahkh</u>·shnayd·uhn <u>lahs</u>·uhn
Not too short.	**Nicht zu kurz.** neekht tsoo koorts
Shorter here.	**Hier kürzer.** heer <u>kewrts</u>·ehr

Sales Help

When do you *open/close*?	**Wann *öffnen/schließen* Sie?** vahn _erf_·nuhn/_shlees_·uhn zee
Where's…?	**Wo ist …?** voh ihst …
– the cashier	**– die Kasse** dee <u>kah</u>·suh
– the escalator	**– die Rolltreppe** dee <u>rohl</u>·trehp·uh
– the elevator [lift]	**– der Fahrstuhl** dehr <u>fahr</u>·shtool
– the fitting room	**– die Umkleidekabine** dee <u>oom</u>·klied·uh·kah·bee·nuh
Can you help me?	**Können Sie mir helfen?** <u>kern</u>·uhn zee meer <u>hehl</u>·fuhn
I'm just looking.	**Ich schaue mich nur um.** eekh <u>show</u>·uh meekh noor oom
I'm already being helped.	**Ich werde schon bedient.** eekh <u>vehrd</u>·uh shohn buh·<u>deent</u>
Do you have…?	**Haben Sie …?** <u>hah</u>·buhn zee …
Can you show me…?	**Können Sie mir … zeigen?** <u>kern</u>·nuhn zee meer … <u>tsieg</u>·uhn
Can you *ship/wrap* it?	**Können Sie das *versenden/einpacken*?** <u>kern</u>·uhn zee dahs _fehr_·<u>zehn</u>·duhn/_<u>ien</u>_·pahk·uhn
How much?	**Wie viel kostet es?** vee feel <u>kohs</u>·tuht ehs
That's all.	**Das ist alles.** dahs ihst <u>ahl</u>·uhs

▶ For clothing items, see page 124.

▶ For food items, see page 84.

▶ For souvenirs, see page 120.

You May Hear...

Kann ich Ihnen helfen? kahn eekh
<u>eehn</u>·uhn <u>hehlf</u>·uhn

Can I help you?

Einen Moment. <u>ien</u>·uhn moh·<u>mehnt</u>

One moment.

Was möchten Sie? vahs <u>merkht</u>·uhn zee

What would you like?

Noch etwas? nohkh <u>eht</u>·vahs

Anything else?

You May See...

GEÖFFNET/GESCHLOSSEN	open/closed
ÜBER MITTAG GESCHLOSSEN	closed for lunch
EINGANG	entrance
UMKLEIDEKABINE	fitting room
KASSE	cashier
NUR BARZAHLUNG MÖGLICH	cash only
KREDITKARTENZAHLUNG MÖGLICH	credit cards accepted
ÖFFNUNGSZEITEN	business hours
AUSGANG	exit

Preferences

I'd like something... **Ich möchte etwas ...** eekh <u>merkht</u>·uh <u>eht</u>·vahs ...

– cheap/expensive **– Billiges/Teueres** <u>bihl</u>·ee·guhs/<u>toy</u>·ehr·uhs

– larger/smaller **– Größeres/Kleineres** <u>grers</u>·eh·ruhs/
<u>klien</u>·eh·ruhs

– nicer **– Schöneres** <u>shern</u>·uh·ruhs

– from this region **– aus dieser Region** ows <u>deez</u>·ehr
rehg·<u>yohn</u>

Around…euros.	**Ungefähr … Euro.** <u>oon</u>·guh·fehr … <u>oy</u>·roh
Is it real?	**Ist das echt?** ihst dahs ehkht
Can you show me…?	**Können Sie mir … zeigen?** <u>kern</u>·uhn zee meer … <u>tsieg</u>·uhn

Decisions

That's not quite what I want.	**Das ist nicht ganz das, was ich möchte.** dahs ihst neekht gahnts dahs vahs eekh <u>merkht</u>·uh
No, I don't like it.	**Das gefällt mir nicht.** dahs guh·<u>fehlt</u> meer neekht
It's too expensive.	**Es ist zu teuer.** ehs ihst tsoo <u>toy</u>·ehr
I have to think about it.	**Das muss ich mir überlegen.** dahs moos eekh meer <u>ewb</u>·ehr·leh·guhn
I'll take it.	**Ich nehme es.** eekh <u>nehm</u>·uh ehs

Bargaining

That's too much.	**Das ist zu viel.** dahs ihst tsoo veel
I'll give you…	**Ich gebe Ihnen …** eekh <u>gehb</u>·uh <u>eehn</u>·uhn …
I have only… euros.	**Ich habe nur … Euro.** eekh <u>hah</u>·buh noor … <u>oy</u>·roh
Is that your best price?	**Ist das Ihr bester Preis?** ihst dahs eehr <u>behst</u>·ehr pries
Can you give me a discount?	**Können Sie mir einen Rabatt geben?** <u>kern</u>·uhn zee meer <u>ien</u>·uhn rah·<u>baht</u> <u>geh</u>·buhn

▶ For numbers, see page 167.

Paying

How much?	**Wie viel kostet es?** vee feel <u>kohs</u>·tuht ehs
I'll pay...	**Ich zahle ...** eekh <u>tsah</u>·luh ...
– in cash	**– bar** bahr
– by credit card	**– mit Kreditkarte** miht kreh·<u>deet</u>·kahr·tuh
– by traveler's check [cheque]	**– mit Reiseschecks** miht <u>riez</u>·uh·shehks
The receipt, please.	**Die Quittung, bitte.** dee <u>kviht</u>·oong <u>biht</u>·tuh

> *i* In Germany, cash is the preferred form of payment. Credit cards are accepted in most larger stores, gas stations, hotels and restaurants. Credit cards may not be accepted by smaller businesses, so be sure to ask before making a purchase. Traveler's checks are not very popular in Germany. If taken, they should be exchanged for cash at a currency exchange office or bank, though a fee will be charged for the exchange. Some banks do not accept traveler's checks.

You May Hear...

Wie möchten Sie zahlen? vee <u>merkht</u>·uhn zee <u>tsahl</u>·uhn	How are you paying?
Ihre Kreditkarte wurde abgelehnt. <u>eehr</u>·uh kreh·<u>deet</u>·kahr·tuh <u>voor</u>·duh <u>ahp</u>·guh·lehnt	Your credit card has been declined.
Ihren Ausweis, bitte. <u>eehr</u>·uhn <u>ows</u>·vies <u>biht</u>·tuh	ID, please.
Wir nehmen keine Kreditkarten. veer <u>neh</u>·muhn <u>kie</u>·nuh kreh·<u>deet</u>·kahr·tuhn	We don't accept credit cards.
Bitte nur Bargeld. <u>biht</u>·tuh noor <u>bahr</u>·gehlt	Cash only, please.
Haben Sie *Wechselgeld/kleine Scheine*? <u>hah</u>·buhn zee *vehkh·zuhl·gehlt/<u>klien</u>·uh <u>shien</u>·uh*	Do you have *change/ small bills [notes]*?

Complaints

I'd like…	**Ich möchte …** eekh <u>merkht</u>·uh …
– to exchange this	**– das umtauschen** dahs <u>oom</u>·tow·shuhn
– a refund	**– gern mein Geld zurück** gehrn mien gehld tsoo·<u>rewk</u>
– to see the manager	**– mit dem Manager sprechen** miht dehm <u>mahn</u>·ah·jehr <u>shprehkh</u>·uhn

Souvenirs

a beer stein	**einen Bierkrug** <u>ien</u>·uh <u>beer</u>·kroog
a bottle of wine	**eine Flasche Wein** <u>ien</u>·uh <u>flahsh</u>·uh vien
a box of chocolates	**eine Schachtel Pralinen** <u>ien</u>·uh <u>shahkht</u>·uhl prah·<u>lee</u>·nuhn
a doll	**eine Puppe** <u>ien</u>·uh <u>poo</u>·puh
a key ring	**ein Schlüsselring** ien <u>shlews</u>·uhl·reeng
a postcard	**eine Postkarte** <u>ien</u>·uh <u>post</u>·kahr·tuh
pottery	**Töpferwaren** <u>terp</u>·fuhr·vah·ruhn
a T-shirt	**ein T-Shirt** ien <u>tee</u>·shehrt
a toy	**ein Spielzeug** ien <u>shpeel</u>·tsoyg

> One of Germany's most famous products is the Black Forest cuckoo clock. Though very expensive, these clocks will last for generations if properly cared for. Another popular and less expensive souvenir is a traditional German beer stein. Collector beer steins are made from clay, glass or pewter and can be brightly painted, with or without a lid and engraved. Germany is also known for its toys: wooden figurines, porcelain dolls and model trains. Other souvenirs include: **Lederhosen** (traditional German pants), lace and porcelain.

Can I see this/that?	**Kann ich das sehen?** kahn eekh dahs <u>zeh</u>·uhn
It's in the *window/display case*.	**Es ist *im Schaufenster/in der Vitrine*.** ehs ihst *ihm <u>schow</u>·fehn·stehr/ihn dehr vih·<u>tree</u>·nuh*
I'd like…	**Ich möchte …** eekh <u>merkht</u>·uh …
– a battery	– **eine Batterie** <u>ien</u>·uh bah·tuh·<u>ree</u>
– a bracelet	– **ein Armband** ien <u>ahrm</u>·bahnt
– a brooch	– **eine Brosche** <u>icn</u>·uh <u>brohsh</u>·uh
– a clock	– **eine Uhr** <u>ien</u>·uh oohr
– earrings	– **Ohrringe** <u>oh</u>·reeng·uh
– a necklace	– **eine Kette** <u>ien</u>·uh <u>keht</u>·uh
– a ring	– **einen Ring** <u>ien</u>·uhn reeng
– a watch	– **eine Uhr** <u>ien</u>·uh oohr

121

I'd like...	**Ich möchte ...** eekh <u>merkht</u>·uh ...
– copper	– **Kupfer** <u>koop</u>·fehr
– crystal	– **Kristall** krihs·<u>tahl</u>
– diamonds	– **Diamanten** dee·ah·<u>mahn</u>·tuhn
– *white/yellow* gold	– *__Weißgold/Gelbgold__* <u>*vies*</u>·*gohlt*/<u>*gehlb*</u>·*gohlt*
– pearls	– **Perlen** <u>pehr</u>·luhn
– pewter	– **Zinn** tsihn
– platinum	– **Platin** <u>plah</u>·teen
– sterling silver	– **Sterlingsilber** <u>shtehr</u>·leeng·<u>zihl</u>·behr
Is this real?	**Ist das echt?** ihst dahs ehkht
Can you engrave it?	**Können Sie etwas eingravieren?** <u>ker</u>·nuhn zee <u>eht</u>·vahs <u>ien</u>·grah·vee·ruhn

Antiques

How old is it?	**Wie alt ist es?** vee ahlt ihst ehs
Do you have anything from the…period?	**Haben Sie etwas aus der ... Zeit?** <u>hah</u>·buhn zee <u>eht</u>·vahs ows dehr ... tsiet
Do I have to fill out any forms?	**Muss ich irgendwelche Formulare ausfüllen?** moos eekh <u>eer</u>·guhnd·vehlkh·uh fohr·moo·<u>lahr</u>·uh <u>ows</u>·fewl·uhn
Is there a certificate of authenticity?	**Gibt es ein Echtheitszeugnis?** gihpt ehs ien <u>ehkht</u>·hiets·tsoyg·nuhs

Clothing

I'd like...	**Ich möchte ...** eekh <u>merkht</u>·uh ...
Can I try this on?	**Kann ich das anprobieren?** kahn eekh dahs <u>ahn</u>·proh·bee·ruhn

It doesn't fit.	**Es passt nicht.** ehs pahst neekht
It's too…	**Es ist zu …** ehs ihst tsoo …
– big/small	**– groß/klein** grohs/klien
– short/long	**– kurz/lang** koorts/lahng
– tight/loose	**– eng/weit** ehng/viet
Do you have this in size…?	**Haben Sie das in der Größe … ?** hah·buhn zee dahs ihn dehr grers·uh …
Do you have this in a *bigger/ smaller* size?	**Haben Sie das in einer *größeren/kleineren* Größe?** hah·buhn zee dahs ihn *ien·ehr grers·ehr·uhn/klien·uh·ruhn* grers·uh

▶ For numbers, see page 167.

You May Hear…

Das steht Ihnen gut. dahs shteht eehn·uhn goot	That looks great on you.
Passt es? pahst ehs	How does it fit?
Wir führen Ihre Größe nicht. veer fewhr·uhn eehr·uh grers·uh neekht	We don't have your size.

You May See…

HERRENABTEILUNG	men's (department)
DAMENABTEILUNG	women's (department)
KINDERABTEILUNG	children's (department)

Color

I'd like something…	**Ich möchte etwas …** eekh <u>merkht</u>·uh <u>eht</u>·vahs …
– beige	**– Beiges** <u>behdj</u>·uhs
– black	**– Schwarzes** <u>shvahrtz</u>·uhs
– blue	**– Blaues** <u>blow</u>·uhs
– brown	**– Braunes** <u>brown</u>·uhs
– green	**– Grünes** <u>grewn</u>·uhs
– gray	**– Graues** <u>grow</u>·uhs
– orange	**– Oranges** <u>oh</u>·rahnj·uhs
– pink	**– Pinkes** <u>peenk</u>·uhs
– purple	**– Violettes** vee·oh·<u>leht</u>·uhs
– red	**– Rotes** <u>roht</u>·uhs
– white	**– Weißes** <u>vies</u>·uhs
– yellow	**– Gelbes** <u>gehlb</u>·uhs

Clothes and Accessories

backpack	**der Rucksack** dehr <u>rook</u>·zahk
belt	**der Gürtel** dehr <u>gewrt</u>·uhl
bikini	**der Bikini** dehr bih·<u>kee</u>·nee
blouse	**die Bluse** dee <u>bloo</u>·zuh
bra	**der BH** dehr beh·<u>hah</u>
briefs [underpants]	**der Schlüpfer** dehr <u>shlewp</u>·fehr
coat	**der Mantel** dehr <u>mahnt</u>·ehl
dress	**das Kleid** dahs klied
hat	**der Hut** dehr hoot
jacket	**die Jacke** dee <u>yah</u>·kuh
jeans	**die Jeans** dee djeens
pajamas	**der Schlafanzug** dehr <u>shlahf</u>·ahn·tsoog

pants [trousers]	**die Hose** dee <u>hohz</u>·uh
pantyhose [tights]	**die Strumpfhose** dee <u>shtroompf</u>·hoh·zuh
purse [handbag]	**die Handtasche** dee <u>hahnd</u>·tahsh·uh
raincoat	**der Regenmantel** dehr <u>rehg</u>·uhn·mahn·tuhl
scarf	**der Schal** dehr shahl
shirt	**das Hemd** dahs hehmt
shorts	**die kurze Hose** dee <u>koortz</u>·uh <u>hohz</u>·uh
skirt	**der Rock** dehr rohk
socks	**die Socken** dee <u>zohk</u>·uhn
suit	**der Anzug** dehr <u>ahn</u>·tsoog
sunglasses	**die Sonnenbrille** dee <u>zohn</u>·uhn·brihl·uh
sweater	**der Pullover** dehr <u>pool</u>·oh·fehr
sweatshirt	**das Sweatshirt** dahs <u>sveht</u>·shehrt
swimsuit	**der Badeanzug** dehr <u>bah</u>·deh·ahn·tsoog
T-shirt	**das T-Shirt** dahs <u>tee</u>·shert
tie	**die Krawatte** dee krah·<u>vah</u>·tuh
underwear	**die Unterwäsche** dee <u>oon</u>·tehr·vehsh·uh

Fabric

I'd like...	**Ich möchte ...** eekh <u>merkht</u>·uh ...
– cotton	**– Baumwolle** <u>bowm</u>·vohl·uh
– denim	**– Denim** <u>dehn</u>·ihm
– lace	**– Spitze** <u>shpihts</u>·uh
– leather	**– Leder** <u>lehd</u>·ehr
– linen	**– Leinen** <u>lien</u>·uhn
– silk	**– Seide** <u>zied</u>·uh
– wool	**– Wolle** <u>vohl</u>·uh
Is it machine washable?	**Ist es waschmaschinenfest?** ihst ehs vahsh·mah·<u>sheen</u>·uhn·fehst

Shoes

I'd like…	**Ich möchte …** eekh <u>merkht</u>·uh …
– *high-heel/flat* shoes	– **Schuhe *mit Absatz/ohne Absatz*** <u>shoo</u>·uh *miht <u>ahp</u>·zahts/<u>ohn</u>·uh <u>ahb</u>·zahts*
– boots	– **Stiefel** <u>shtee</u>·fuhl
– loafers	– **Slipper** <u>slihp</u>·ehr
– sandals	– **Sandalen** zahn·<u>dahl</u>·uhn
– shoes	– **Schuhe** <u>shoo</u>·uh
– slippers	– **Badelatschen** <u>bah</u>·duh·lahtsh·uhn
– sneakers	– **Turnschuhe** <u>toorn</u>·shoo·huh
In size…	**In der Größe …** ihn dehr <u>grers</u>·uh …

▶For numbers, see page 167.

Sizes

small (S)	**klein** klein
medium (M)	**mittel** <u>miht</u>·tuhl
large (L)	**gross** grohs
extra large (XL)	**extra gross** <u>ehks</u>·trah grohs

In addition to small, medium and large, many clothing articles are labeled by Continental size. As that size varies by manufacturer, be sure to try on any article before buying.

Newsstand and Tobacconist

Do you sell English-language newspapers?	**Haben Sie englischsprachige Zeitungen?** <u>hah</u>·buhn zee <u>ehng</u>·leesh·shprah·khee·guh <u>tsie</u>·toong·uhn
I'd like…	**Ich möchte …** eekh <u>merkht</u>·uh …
– candy [sweets]	– **Süßigkeiten** <u>zews</u>·eekh·kiet·uhn
– chewing gum	– **Kaugummi** <u>kow</u>·goo·mee

126

– a chocolate bar	– **einen Schokoladenriegel** <u>ien</u>·uhn shoh·koh·<u>lahd</u>·uhn·ree·guhl
– a cigar	– **eine Zigarre** <u>ien</u>·uh tsee·<u>gahr</u>·uh
– a *pack/carton* of cigarettes	– **eine *Schachtel/Stange* Zigaretten** <u>ien</u>·uh *<u>shahkht</u>·uhl/<u>shtahng</u>·uh* tsee·gahr·<u>eht</u>·uhn
– a lighter	– **ein Feuerzeug** ien <u>foy</u>·ehr·tsoyg
– a magazine	– **eine Zeitschrift** <u>ien</u>·uh <u>tsiet</u>·shrihft
– matches	– **Streichhölzer** <u>shtriekh</u>·herlts·uhr
– a newspaper	– **eine Zeitung** <u>ien</u>·uh <u>tsie</u>·toong
– a pen	– **einen Stift** <u>ien</u>·uhn shtihft
– a postcard	– **eine Postkarte** <u>ien</u>·uh <u>pohst</u>·kahr·tuh
– a *road/town* map of…	– *eine Straßenkarte/ einen Stadtplan* **vonen** … <u>ien</u>·uh *<u>shtrahsuhn</u>·kahrt·uh/<u>ien</u>·uhn <u>shtaht</u>·plahn* fohn …
– stamps	– **Briefmarken** <u>breef</u>·mahrk·uhn

Photography

I'd like a/an… camera.	**Ich möchte eine … Kamera.** eekh <u>merkht</u>·uh <u>ien</u>·uh … <u>kah</u>·meh·ruh
– automatic	– **automatische** ow·toh·<u>maht</u>·ihsh·uh
– digital	– **digitale** <u>dihd</u>·juh·tuhl
– disposable	– **Wegwerf-** <u>vehk</u>·vehrf-
I'd like…	**Ich möchte …** eekh <u>merkht</u>·uh …
– a battery	– **eine Batterie** <u>ien</u>·uh bah·tuh·<u>ree</u>
– digital prints	– **digitale Ausdrucke** <u>dihd</u>·juh·tuhl <u>ows</u>·drook·uh
– a memory card	– **eine Speicherkarte** <u>ien</u>·uh <u>shpie</u>·khuhr·kahrt·uh
Can I print digital photos here?	**Kann ich hier Digitalfotos ausdrucken lassen?** kahn eekh heer dihd·jih·<u>tahl</u>·foh·tohs <u>ows</u>·droo·kuhn <u>lahs</u>·uhn

Sports and Leisure

Essential

When's the game?	**Wann findet das Spiel statt?** vahn <u>fihnd</u>·uht dahs shpeel shtaht
Where's...?	**Wo ist ... ?** voh ihst ...
– the beach	**– der Strand** dehr shtrahnd
– the park	**– der Park** dehr pahrk
– the pool	**– der Pool** dehr pool
Is it safe to swim here?	**Kann man hier schwimmen?** kahn mahn heer <u>shvihm</u>·uhn
Can I rent [hire] golf clubs?	**Kann ich Golfschläger ausleihen?** kahn eekh gohlf·<u>shlelig</u>·ehr <u>ows</u>·lie·uhn
How much per hour?	**Wie viel kostet es pro Stunde?** vee feel <u>kohs</u>·tuht ehs proh <u>shtoond</u>·uh
How far is it to...?	**Wie weit ist es bis zum♂/zur♀ ...?** vee viet ihst ehs bihs tsoom♂/tsoor♀ ...
Show me on the map, please.	**Zeigen Sie es mir bitte auf dem Stadtplan.** <u>tsieg</u>·uhn zee ehs meer <u>biht</u>·tuh owf dehm <u>shtaht</u>·plahn

Spectator Sports

When's...?	**Wann findet ... statt?** vahn <u>fihnd</u>·uht ... shtaht
– the baseball game	**– das Baseballspiel** dahs <u>behs</u>·bahl·shpeel
– the basketball game	**– das Basketballspiel** dahs <u>bahs</u>·kuht·bahl·shpeel
– the boxing match	**– der Boxkampf** dehr <u>bohx</u>·kahmpf
– the cricket match	**– das Cricket-Turnier** dahs <u>krih</u>·kuht·toor·neer

– the cycling race	**das Radrennen** dahs <u>rahd</u>·rehn·uhn
– the golf tournament	**das Golfturnier** dahs <u>gohlf</u>·toor·neer
– the soccer [football] game	**das Fußballspiel** dahs <u>foos</u>·bahl·shpeel
– the tennis match	**das Tennismatch** dahs <u>tehn</u>·ihs·mahch
– the volleyball game	**das Volleyballspiel** dahs <u>voh</u>·lee·bahl·shpeel
Who's playing?	**Wer spielt?** vehr shpeelt
Where's the *racetrack/stadium*?	**Wo ist *die Rennbahn/das Stadion*?** voh ihst dee <u>rehn</u>·bahn/dahs <u>shtah</u>·dyohn
Where can I place a bet?	**Wo kann ich eine Wette abschließen?** voh kahn eekh <u>ien</u>·uh <u>veh</u>·tuh <u>ahp</u>·shlees·uhn

▶ For ticketing, see page 19.

i

Germany's most popular sport is **Fußball** (soccer); in fact, Germany has won the World Cup three times. Tennis is another popular sport; the German Tennis Federation boasts membership of more than one million. Other popular sports include biking, hiking, handball, basketball, volleyball, ice hockey, golf and horseback riding.

Casinos are found throughout Germany. The spa towns, in particular, are home to well-known casinos.

Participating

Where *is/are*...?	**Wo *ist/sind* ...?** voh *ihst/zihnt* ...
– the golf course	**– der Golfplatz** dehr <u>gohlf</u>·plahts
– the gym	**– die Sporthalle** dee <u>shpohrt</u>·hah·luh
– the park	**– der Park** dehr pahrk
– the tennis courts	**– die Tennisplätze** dee <u>tehn</u>·ihs·pleht·suh

How much per…	**Wie viel kostet es pro …** vee feel kohs·tuht ehs proh …
– day	**– Tag** tak
– hour	**– Stunde** shtoond·uh
– game	**– Spiel** shpeel
– round	**– Runde** roond·uh
Can I rent [hire]…?	**Kann ich … ausleihen?** kahn eekh … ows·lie·huhn
– golf clubs	**– Golfschläger** gohlf·shlehg·ehr
– equipment	**– eine Ausrüstung** ien·uh ows·rews·toong
– a racket	**– einen Schläger** ien·uhn shlehg·ehr

At the Beach/Pool

Where's the *beach/pool*?	**Wo ist der *Strand/Pool*?** voh ihst dehr *shtrahnt/pool*
Is there a…?	**Gibt es einen …?** gihpt ehs ien·uhn …
– kiddie pool	**– Pool für Kinder** pool fewr kihnd·ehr
– *indoor/outdoor* pool	**– *Hallenbad/Freibad*** hahl·ehn·baht/frie·baht
– lifeguard	**– Rettungsschwimmer** reht·oongs·shvihm·ehr
Is it safe to *swim/dive*?	**Ist es sicher zu *schwimmen/tauchen*?** ihst ehs sihk·hehr tsoo *shvihm·uhn/towkh·uhn*
Is it safe for children?	**Ist es kindgerecht?** ihst ehs kihnt·guh·rehkht

▶ For travel with children, see page 142.

I'd like to rent [hire]…	**Ich möchte gern … ausleihen.** eekh merkht·uh gehrn … ows·lie·uhn
– a deck chair	**– einen Liegestuhl** ien·uhn leeg·uh·shtool
– diving equipment	**– eine Tauchausrüstung** ien·uh towkh·ows·rew·stoong
– a jet ski	**– einen Jet Ski** ien·uhn djeht skee
– a motorboat	**– ein Motorboot** ien moht·ohr·boht

– a rowboat	– **ein Ruderboot** ien <u>rood</u>·ehr·boht
– snorkeling equipment	– **eine Schnorchelausrüstung** <u>ien</u>·uh <u>shnohr</u>·khehl·ows·rew·stoong
– a surfboard	– **ein Surfboard** ien <u>soorf</u>·bohrd
– a towel	– **ein Handtuch** ien <u>hahnd</u>·tookh
– an umbrella	– **einen Schirm** <u>ien</u>·uhn sheerm
– water skis	– **Wasserski** <u>vahs</u>·ehr·shee
– a windsurfer	– **ein Surfbrett** ien serf·breht
For…hours.	**Für … Stunden.** fewr … <u>shtoond</u>·uhn

> Germany's main beach areas are located along the North Sea and Baltic Sea coasts. There are numerous types of beaches in Germany, including family, adults-only and nude beaches. A few of the more popular areas include Sylt, known for its nude beaches; Büsum, an intimate small town with calm North Sea waters; Helgoland, a Frisian island in the North Sea; Heiligendamm, Germany's oldest seaside resort; Heringsdorf, on the island of Usedom; and Kühlungsborn and Warnemünde, located on the Baltic Sea.

Winter Sports

A lift pass for *a day/ five days*, please.	**Einen Liftpass für *einen Tag/fünf Tage*, bitte.** <u>ien</u>·uhn <u>lihft</u>·pahs fewr <u>ien</u>·uhn tahk/fewnf <u>tahg</u>·uh <u>biht</u>·tuh
I'd like to rent [hire]…	**Ich möchte gerne … ausleihen.** eekh <u>merkht</u>·uh <u>gehr</u>·nuh … <u>ows</u>·lle·uhn
– boots	– **Stiefel** <u>shteef</u>·uhl
– a helmet	– **einen Helm** <u>ien</u>·uhn hehlm
– poles	– **Stöcke** <u>shterk</u>·uh
– skis	– **Skier** <u>skee</u>·ehr
– a snowboard	– **ein Snowboard** ien <u>snohw</u>·bohrd
– snowshoes	– **Schneeschuhe** <u>shneh</u>·shoo·uh

These are too big/small.	**Diese sind zu *groß/klein.*** <u>dee</u>·zuh zihnt tsoo *grohs/klien*
Are there lessons?	**Kann man Stunden nehmen?** kahn mahn <u>shtoond</u>·uhn <u>neh</u>·muhn
I'm a beginner.	**Ich bin Anfänger.** eekh bihn ahn·<u>fehng</u>·ehr
I'm experienced.	**Ich bin erfahren.** eekh been ehr·<u>fahr</u>·uhn
A trail [piste] map, please.	**Bitte einen Pistenplan.** <u>biht</u>·tuh <u>ien</u>·uhn <u>pees</u>·tuhn·plahn

You May See...

SCHLEPPLIFT	drag lift
SEILBAHN	cable car
SESSELLIFT	chair lift
ANFÄNGER	novice
FORTGESCHRITTENE	intermediate
KÖNNER	expert
PISTE GESCHLOSSEN	trail [piste] closed

i Winter offers plenty of opportunities for outdoor activity in Germany. Alpine skiing, snowboarding, cross-country skiing, ice skating, tobogganing and hiking are just some of the options available to winter travelers.

In the Countryside

A map of..., please.	**Eine Karte ..., bitte.** <u>ien</u>·uh <u>kahrt</u>·uh ... <u>biht</u>·tuh
– this region	**– dieser Region** <u>deez</u>·uhr rehg·<u>yohn</u>
– the walking routes	**– mit Wanderrouten** miht <u>vahnd</u>·ehr·root·uhn
– the bike routes	**– mit Radrouten** miht <u>rahd</u>·root·uhn
– the trails	**– mit Wanderwegen** miht <u>vahnd</u>·ehr·veh·guhn
Is it...?	**Ist es ...?** ihst ehs ...
– easy	**– leicht** liekht
– difficult	**– schwierig** <u>shveer</u>·eeg
– far	**– weit** viet
– steep	**– steil** shtiel
How far is it to...?	**Wie weit ist es bis ...?** vee viet ihst ehs bihs ...

Show me on the map, please.	**Zeigen Sie es mir bitte auf der Karte.** tsieg·uhn zee ehs meer biht·tuh owf dehr kahrt·uh
I'm lost.	**Ich habe mich verlaufen.** eekh hahb·uh meekh fehr·lowf·uhn
Where's...?	**Wo ist ...?** voh ihst ...
– the bridge	– **die Brücke** dee brew·kuh
– the cave	– **die Höhle** dee her·luh
– the canyon	– **der Canyon** dehr kahn·yohn
– the cliff	– **die Klippe** dee klih·puh
– the farm	– **der Bauernhof** dehr bow·ehrn·hohf
– the field	– **das Feld** dahs fehld
– the forest	– **der Wald** dehr vahld
– the hill	– **der Hügel** dehr hew·gehl
– the lake	– **der See** dehr zeh
– the mountain	– **der Berg** dehr behrg
– the nature preserve	– **das Naturschutzgebiet** dahs nah·toor·shoots·guh·beet
– the overlook [viewpoint]	– **der Aussichtspunkt** dehr ows·seekhts·poonkt
– the park	– **der Park** dehr pahrk
– the path	– **der Pfad** dehr pfahd
– the peak	– **der Gipfel** dehr gihp·fuhl
– the picnic area	– **der Picknickplatz** dehr pihk·nihk·plahts
– the pond	– **der Teich** dehr tiekh
– the ravine	– **die Schlucht** dee shlookht
– the river	– **der Fluss** dehr floos
– the sea	– **das Meer** dahs mehr
– the (hot) spring	– **die (heiße) Quelle** dee (hie·suh) kveh·luh
– the stream	– **der Strom** dehr shtrom

– the valley	– **das Tal** dahs tahl
– the village	– **das Dorf** dahs dohrf
– the vineyard	– **das Weingut** dahs <u>vien</u>·goot
– the waterfall	– **der Wasserfall** dehr <u>vahs</u>·ehr·fahl

Culture and Nightlife

Essential

What's there to do at night?	**Was kann man dort abends unternehmen?** vahs kahn mahn dohrt <u>ahb</u>·uhnds oon·tehr·<u>nehm</u>·uhn
Do you have a program of events?	**Haben Sie ein Veranstaltungsprogramm?** <u>hah</u>·buhn zee ien fehr·<u>ahn</u>·shtahlt·oongs·prohg·rahm
What's playing tonight?	**Was wird heute Abend aufgeführt?** vahs vihrd <u>hoyt</u>·uh <u>ahb</u>·uhnd <u>owf</u>·guh·fewrt
Where's...?	**Wo ist ...?** voh ihst ...
– the downtown area	– **das Stadtzentrum** dahs <u>shtadt</u>·tsehn·troom
– the bar	– **die Bar** dee bahr
– the dance club	– **der Tanzclub** dee <u>tahnts</u>·kloop
Is there a cover charge?	**Kostet es Eintritt?** <u>kohs</u>·tuht ehs <u>ien</u>·triht

Entertainment

Can you recommend...?	**Können Sie ... empfehlen?** <u>kern</u>·uhn zee ... ehm·<u>pfeh</u>·luhn
– a concert	– **ein Konzert** ien kohn·<u>tsehrt</u>
– a movie	– **einen Film** <u>ien</u>·uhn feelm
– an opera	– **eine Oper** <u>ien</u>·uhn <u>oh</u>·pehr
– a play	– **ein Theaterstück** ien teh·<u>ah</u>·tehr·shtewk

When does it start/end?	**Wann *beginnt/endet* es?** vahn *beh·<u>gihnt</u>/ <u>ehnd</u>·eht* ehs
Where's...?	**Wo ist ...?** voh ihst ...
– the concert hall	**– die Konzerthalle** dee kohn·<u>tsehrt</u>·hah·luh
– the opera house	**– das Opernhaus** dahs <u>oh</u>·pehrn·hows
– the theater	**– das Theater** dahs teh·<u>ah</u>·tehr
What's the dress code?	**Wie ist die Kleiderordnung?** vee ihst dee <u>klied</u>·ehr·ohrd·noong
I like...	**Mir gefällt ...** meer guh·<u>fehlt</u> ...
– classical music	**– klassische Musik** <u>klahs</u>·ihsh·uh moo·<u>zeek</u>
– folk music	**– Volksmusik** <u>fohlks</u>·moo·zeek
– jazz	**– Jazz** djehz
– pop music	**– Popmusik** <u>pohp</u>·moo·zeek
– rap	**– Rap** rehp

▶ For ticketing, see page 19.

i Listings of regional events can be found in local newspapers. The local tourist information office and your hotel concierge can be useful sources of information about local events, and may also be able to help you obtain tickets and plan transportation.

You May Hear...

Bitte schalten Sie Ihre Handys aus.
biht·tuh shahlt·uhn zee eehr·uh hehnd·ees ows

Turn off your cell [mobile] phones, please.

Nightlife

What's there to do at night?	**Was kann man dort abends unternehmen?** vahs kahn mahn dohrt ahb·uhnds oont·ehr·nehm·uhn
Can you recommend...?	**Können Sie ... empfehlen?** kern·uhn zee ... ehm·pfeh·luhn
– a bar	**– eine Bar** ien·uh bahr
– a casino	**– ein Casino** ien kah·see·noh
– a dance club	**– einen Tanzclub** ien·uhn tahnts·kloop
– a gay club	**– einen Schwulenclub** ien·uhn shvoo·luhn·kloop
– a jazz club	**– einen Jazzclub** ien·uhn yahts·kloop
Is there live music?	**Gibt es dort Livemusik?** gihpt ehs dohrt liev·moo·zeek
How do I get there?	**Wie komme ich dorthin?** vee kohm·uh eekh dohrt·hihn
Is there a cover charge?	**Kostet es Eintritt?** kohs·tuht ehs ien·triht
Let's go dancing.	**Lass uns tanzen gehen.** ahs oons tahnt·suhn geh·uhn

▼ Special Needs

Business Travel

Essential

I'm here on business.	**Ich bin geschäftlich hier.** eekh been guh·*shehft*·leekh heer
Here's my business card.	**Hier ist meine Visitenkarte.** heer ihst <u>mien</u>·uh vih·<u>zee</u>·tuhn·kahr·tuh
Can I have your card?	**Kann ich Ihre Karte haben?** kahn eekh <u>ihhr</u>·uh <u>kahrt</u>·uh hah·buhn
I have a meeting with…	**Ich habe ein Meeting mit …** eekh <u>hahb</u>·uh ien <u>mee</u>·teeng miht …
Where's the *convention hall/ meeting room*?	**Wo ist *der Kongresssaal/das Konferenzzimmer*?** voh ihst *dehr kohn·<u>grehs</u>·sahl/dahs kohn·fehr·<u>ehnts</u>·tsihm·ehr*

> Germans are generally formal and so are their greetings. Business introductions are always accompanied by a handshake. Address business colleagues by title: **Herr** (Mr.), **Frau** (Miss/Ms./Mrs.) or **Herr Dr.** (Dr.) and the person's last name. **Herr Professor** and **Frau Professor** are also used, but usually without a last name.

Business Communication

I'm here for…	**Ich bin für … hier.** eekh been fuer … heer
– a seminar	– **ein Seminar** ien zehm·ee·<u>nahr</u>
– a conference	– **eine Konferenz** <u>ien</u>·uh kohn·feh·<u>rehnts</u>
– a meeting	– **ein Meeting** ien <u>mee</u>·teeng
My name is…	**Mein Name ist …** mien <u>nahm</u>·uh ihst …
May I introduce my colleague…?	**Darf ich Ihnen meinen Kollegen … vorstellen?** dahrf eekh <u>eehn</u>·uhn <u>mien</u>·uhn koh·<u>leh</u>·guhn … <u>fohr</u>·shtehl·uhn

I have *a meeting/an appointment* with…	**Ich habe *ein Meeting/einen Termin* mit …** eekh <u>hahb</u>·uh *ien <u>mee</u>·teeng/<u>ien</u>·uhn tehr·<u>meen</u>* miht …
I'm sorry I'm late.	**Es tut mir leid, dass ich spät bin.** ehs toot meer lied dahs eekh shpayt bihn
I need an interpreter.	**Ich brauche einen Dolmetscher.** eek <u>browkh</u>·uh <u>ien</u>·uhn <u>dohl</u>·meh·chehr
You can reach me at the…Hotel.	**Sie können mich im … Hotel erreichen.** zee <u>kern</u>·uhn meekh ihm … hoh·<u>tehl</u> ehr·<u>riekh</u>·uhn
I'm here until…	**Ich bin bis … hier.** eekh bihn bihs … heer
I need to…	**Ich muss …** eekh moos …
– make a call	**– telefonieren** tehl·eh·fohn·<u>eer</u>·uhn
– make a photocopy	**– eine Kopie machen** <u>ien</u>·uh <u>koh</u>·pee·uh <u>mahkh</u>·uhn
– send an e-mail	**– eine E-Mail senden** <u>ien</u>·uh <u>ee</u>·mehl <u>zehnd</u>·uhn
– send a fax	**– ein Fax senden** ien fahx <u>zehnd</u>·uhn
– send a package (overnight)	**– ein Paket schicken (per Express)** ien pah·<u>keht</u> <u>shihk</u>·uhn (pehr <u>ehks</u>·prehs)
It was a pleasure to meet you.	**Es war schön, Sie kennenzulernen.** ehs vahr shern zee <u>keh</u>·nehn·tsoo·lehr·nehn

▶For internet and communications, see page 49.

You May Hear...

Haben Sie einen Termin?
<u>hah</u>·buhn zee <u>ien</u>·uhn tehr·<u>meen</u>

Do you have
an appointment?

Mit wem? meet vehm

With whom?

Er♂/Sie♀ ist in einem Meeting.
ehr♂/zee♀ ihst ihn <u>ien</u>·uhm <u>mee</u>·teeng

He/She is in
a meeting.

Einen Moment, bitte.
<u>ien</u>·uhn moh·<u>mehnt</u> <u>biht</u>·tuh

One moment,
please.

Nehmen Sie Platz. <u>nehm</u>·uhn zee plats

Have a seat.

Möchten Sie etwas zu trinken?
<u>merkht</u>·uhn zee <u>eht</u>·vahs tsoo <u>trihnk</u>·uhn

Would you like
something to drink?

Vielen Dank für Ihr Kommen.
<u>feel</u>·uhn dahnk fewr eehr <u>kohm</u>·uhn

Thank you for
coming.

Travel with Children

Essential

Is there a discount for kids?	**Gibt es Ermäßigung für Kinder?** gihpt ehs ehr·meh·see·goong fewr kihn·dehr
Can you recommend a babysitter?	**Können Sie einen Babysitter empfehlen?** kern·uhn zee ien·uhn beh·bee·siht·ehr ehm·pfeh·luhn
Do you have a *child's seat/highchair*?	**Haben Sie einen *Kindersitz/Kinderstuhl*?** hah·buhn zee ien·uhn kihnd·ehr·zihts/ kihnd·ehr·shtoohl
Where can I change the baby?	**Wo kann ich das Baby wickeln?** voh kahn eekh dahs beh·bee vihk·uhln

Fun with Kids

Can you recommend something for kids?	**Können Sie etwas für Kinder empfehlen?** kern·uhn zee eht·vahs fewr kihnd·ehr ehm·pfeh·luhn
Where's…?	**Wo ist …?** voh ihst …
– the amusement park	**– der Vergnügungspark** dehr fehrg·new·goongs·pahrk
– the kiddie [paddling] pool	**– das Kinderbecken** dahs kihnd·ehr·beh·kuhn
– the park	**– der Park** dehr pahrk
– the playground	**– der Spielplatz** dehr shpeel·plats
– the zoo	**– der Zoo** dehr tsoh
Are kids allowed?	**Sind Kinder erlaubt?** zihnt kihnd·ehr ehr·lowbt

Is it safe for kids?	**Ist es für Kinder geeignet?** ihst ehs fewr <u>kihnd</u>·ehr guh·<u>ieg</u>·nuht
Is it suitable for… year olds?	**Ist es für … Jahre alte Kinder geeignet?** ihst ehs fewr … <u>yah</u>·ruh <u>ahlt</u>·uh <u>kihnd</u>·ehr guh·<u>ieg</u>·nuht

▶ For numbers, see page 167.

You May Hear…

Wie süß! vee zews	How cute!
Wie heißt er/sie? vee hiest ehr ♂ /zee ♀	What's his/her name?
Wie alt ist er ♂ /sie ♀ ? vee ahlt ihst ehr ♂ /zee ♀	How old is he/she?

Basic Needs for Kids

Do you have…?	**Haben Sie …?** <u>hah</u>·buhn zee …
– a baby bottle	**– eine Babyflasche** <u>ien</u>·uh beh·bee·<u>flahsh</u>·uh
– baby food	**– Babynahrung** <u>beh</u>·bee·nahr·oong
– baby wipes	**– feuchte Babytücher** <u>foykh</u>·tuh beh·bee·tewkh·ehr
– a car seat	**– einen Kindersitz** <u>ien</u>·uhn <u>kihnd</u>·ehr·zihts
– a children's menu/ a children's portion	**– ein Kindermenü/eine Kinderportion** <u>ien</u>·uhn <u>kihnd</u>·ehr·meh·new/<u>ien</u>·uh <u>kihnd</u>·ehr·pohrtz·yohn·uhn

▶ For dining with kids, see page 65.

– a *child's seat/ highchair*	**– einen *Kindersitz/Kinderstuhl*** <u>ien</u>·uhn <u>kihnd</u>·ehr·zihts/<u>kihnd</u>·ehr·shtoohl
– a *crib/cot*	**– ein *Gitterbett/Kinderbett*** ien <u>giht</u>·tehr·beht/<u>kihnd</u>·ehr·beht
– diapers [nappies]	**– Windeln** <u>vihnd</u>·uhln
– formula [baby food]	**– Babynahrung** <u>beh</u>·bee·nah·roong
– a pacifier [soother]	**– einen Schnuller** <u>ien</u>·uhn <u>shnool</u>·ehr
– a playpen	**– einen Laufstall** <u>ien</u>·uhn <u>lowf</u>·shtahl
– a stroller [pushchair]	**– einen Kinderwagen** <u>ien</u>·uhn <u>kihnd</u>·ehr·vahg·uhn
Can I breastfeed the baby here?	**Kann ich das Baby hier stillen?** kahn eekh dahs <u>beh</u>·bee heer <u>shtihl</u>·uhn
Where can I *breastfeed/change* the baby?	**Wo kann ich das Baby *stillen/wickeln*?** voh kahn eekh dahs <u>beh</u>·bee <u>shtihl</u>·uhn/<u>vihk</u>·uhln

Babysitting

Can you recommend a babysitter?	**Können Sie einen Babysitter empfehlen?** <u>kern</u>·uhn zee <u>ien</u>·uhn <u>beh</u>·bee·siht·ehr ehm·<u>pfeh</u>·luhn
What is the cost?	**Was sind die Kosten?** vahs zihnt dee <u>kohs</u>·tuhn
I'll be back by...	**Ich bin um ... zurück.** eekh been oom ... tsoo·<u>rewk</u>

▶ For time, see page 169.

I can be reached at...	**Ich bin unter ... zu erreichen.** eekh been <u>oont</u>·ehr ... tsoo ehr·<u>riekh</u>·uhn

Health and Emergency

Can you recommend a pediatrician?	**Können Sie einen Kinderarzt empfehlen?** <u>kern</u>·uhn zee <u>ien</u>·uhn <u>kihnd</u>·ehr·ahrtst ehm·<u>pfeh</u>·luhn
My child is allergic to...	**Mein Kind ist allergisch auf ...** mien kihnt ihst ah·<u>lehrg</u>·eesh owf ...
My child is missing.	**Mein Kind ist weg.** mien kihnt ihst vehk
Have you seen a *boy/girl*?	**Haben Sie *einen Jungen/ein Mädchen* gesehen?** <u>hah</u>·buhn zee *<u>ien</u>·uhn <u>yoong</u>·uhn/ien <u>meht</u>·khuhn* guh·<u>zeh</u>·uhn

▶ For food items, see page 84.

▶ For health, see page 152.

▶ For police, see page 149.

For the Disabled

Essential

Is there…?	**Gibt es …?** gihpt ehs …
– access for the disabled	**– einen Zugang für Behinderte** <u>ien</u>·uhn <u>tsoo</u>·gahng fewr beh·<u>hihnd</u>·ehrt·uh
– a wheelchair ramp	**– eine Rollstuhlrampe** <u>ien</u>·uh <u>rohl</u>·shtool·rahm·puh
– a handicapped- [disabled-] accessible toilet	**– eine Behindertentoilette** <u>ien</u>·uh beh·<u>hihn</u>·dehrt·uhn·toy·leh·tuh
I need…	**Ich brauche …** eekh <u>browkh</u>·uh …
– assistance	**– Hilfe** <u>hihlf</u>·uh
– an elevator [a lift]	**– einen Fahrstuhl** <u>ien</u>·uhn <u>fahr</u>·shtoohl
– a ground-floor room	**– ein Zimmer im Erdgeschoss** ien <u>tsihm</u>·ehr ihm <u>ehrd</u>·guh·shohs

Getting Help

I'm…	**Ich bin …** eekh bihn …
– disabled	**– behindert** beh·<u>hihn</u>·dehrt
– visually impaired	**– sehbehindert** <u>zeh</u>·buh·hihn·dehrt
– hearing impaired/ deaf	**– hörgeschädigt/taub** <u>her</u>·guh·sheh·deegt/towb
I'm unable to *walk far/use the stairs.*	**Ich kann nicht *weit laufen/die Treppe benutzen.*** eekh kahn neekht *viet <u>low</u>·fuhn/dee <u>trehp</u>·uh beh·<u>noot</u>·suhn*
Please speak louder.	**Bitte sprechen Sie lauter.** <u>biht</u>·tuh <u>shprehkh</u>·uhn zee <u>lowt</u>·ehr

Eingang

Can I bring my wheelchair?	**Kann ich meinen Rollstuhl mitbringen?** kahn eekh <u>mien</u>•uhn <u>rohl</u>•shtoohl <u>miht</u>•brihng•uhn
Are guide dogs permitted?	**Sind Blindenhunde erlaubt?** zihnt <u>blihnd</u>•uhn•hoond•uh ehr•<u>lowbt</u>
Can you help me?	**Können Sie mir helfen?** <u>kern</u>•uhn zee meer <u>hehlf</u>•uhn
Please *open/hold* the door.	**Bitte *öffnen/halten* Sie die Tür.** <u>biht</u>•tuh *<u>erf</u>•nuhn/<u>hahlt</u>•uhn* zee dee tewr

▼ *Resources*

Emergencies

Essential

Help!	**Hilfe!** <u>hihlf</u>·uh
Go away!	**Gehen Sie weg!** <u>geh</u>·uhn zee vehk
Stop, thief!	**Haltet den Dieb!** <u>hahlt</u>·uht dehn deeb
Get a doctor!	**Holen Sie einen Arzt!** <u>hohl</u>·uhn zee <u>ien</u>·uhn ahrtst
Fire!	**Feuer!** <u>foy</u>·ehr
I'm lost.	**Ich habe mich verlaufen.** eekh <u>hahb</u>·uh meekh fehr·<u>lowf</u>·uhn
Can you help me?	**Können Sie mir helfen?** <u>kern</u>·uhn zee meer <u>hehlf</u>·uhn

Police

Essential

Call the police!	**Rufen Sie die Polizei!** <u>roof</u>·uhn zee dee poh·leet·<u>sie</u>
Where's the police station?	**Wo ist das Polizeirevier?** voh ihst dahs poh·leet·<u>sie</u>·ruh·veer
There was an *accident/attack*.	**Es gab einen *Unfall/Überfall*.** ehs gahb <u>ien</u>·uhn <u>oon</u>·fahl/<u>ewb</u>·ehr·fahl
My child is missing.	**Mein Kind ist weg.** mien kihnt ihst vehk
I need an interpreter.	**Ich brauche einen Dolmetscher.** eekh <u>browkh</u>·uh <u>ien</u>·uhn <u>dohl</u>·mech·ehr

I need *to contact my lawyer/make a phone call.*	**Ich muss *mit meinem Anwalt sprechen/ telefonieren.*** eekh moos *miht mien·uhm ahn·vahlt shpreh·khehn/tehl·eh·fohn·eer·uhn*
I'm innocent.	**Ich bin unschuldig.** eekh bihn oon·shoold·eekh

You May Hear...

Füllen Sie dieses Formular aus. fewl·uhn zee deez·uhs fohr·moo·lahr ows	Fill out this form.
Ihren Ausweis, bitte. eehr·uhn ows·vies biht·tuh	Your identification, please.
***Wann/Wo* ist es passiert?** *vahn/voh* ihst ehs pah·seert	*When/Where* did it happen?
Wie sah er♂/sie♀ aus? vee zah ehr♂/zee♀ ows	What does he/she look like?

Contact your consulate, ask the concierge at your hotel, or ask the tourist information office for telephone numbers of the local ambulance, emergency services and police.

Lost Property and Theft

I'd like to report…	**Ich möchte … melden.**	eekh _merkht_·uh … _mehld_·uhn
– a mugging	**– einen Überfall**	_ien_·uhn _ewb_·ehr·fahl
– a rape	**– eine Vergewaltigung**	_ien_·uh fehr·guh·_vahlt_·ee·goong
– a theft	**– einen Diebstahl**	_ien_·uhn _deeb_·shtahl
I was _mugged/robbed_.	**Ich wurde _überfallen/beraubt_.**	eekh _voor_·duh _ewb·ehr·fahl_·uhn/beh·_rowbt_
I lost…	**Ich habe … verloren.**	eekh _hahb_·uh … fehr·_lohr_·uhn
…was stolen.	**… wurde gestohlen.**	… _voor_·duh geh·_shtohl_·uhn
– My backpack	**– Mein Rucksack**	mien _rook_·zahk
– My bicycle	**– Mein Fahrrad**	mien _fahr_·ahd
– My camera	**– Meine Kamera**	_mien_·uh _kah_·meh·rah
– My rental [hire] car	**– Mein Mietauto**	mien _meet_·ow·toh
– My computer	**– Mein Computer**	mien kohm·_pjoo_·tehr
– My credit card	**– Meine Kreditkarte**	_mien_·uh kreh·_deet_·kahrt·uh
– My jewelry	**– Mein Schmuck**	mien shmook
– My money	**– Mein Geld**	mien gehlt
– My passport	**– Mein Reisepass**	mien _riez_·uh·pahs
– My purse [handbag]	**– Meine Handtasche**	_mien_·uh _hahnd_·tahsh·uh
– My traveler's checks [cheques]	**– Meine Reisechecks**	_mien_·uh _riez_·uh·shehks
– My wallet	**– Meine Brieftasche**	_mien_·uh _breef_·tahsh·uh
I need a police report.	**Ich brauche einen Polizeibericht.**	eekh _browkh_·uh _ien_·uhn poh·leet·_sie_·beh·reekht

Essential

I'm sick [ill].	**Ich bin krank.** eekh bihn krahnk
I need an English-speaking doctor.	**Ich brauche einen englischsprechenden Arzt.** eekh <u>browkh</u>·uh <u>ien</u>·uhn <u>ehng</u>·glihsh·shprehkh·ehnd·uhn ahrtst
It hurts here.	**Es tut hier weh.** ehs toot heer veh
I have a stomachache.	**Ich habe Magenschmerzen.** eekh <u>hahb</u>·uh <u>mahg</u>·uhn·shmehrt·suhn

Finding a Doctor —————————————

Can you recommend a *doctor/dentist*?	**Können Sie einen *Arzt/Zahnarzt* empfehlen?** <u>kern</u>·uhn zee <u>ien</u>·uhn *ahrtst/ tsahn·ahrtst* ehm·<u>pfeh</u>·luhn
Can the doctor come here?	**Kann der Arzt herkommen?** kahn dehr ahrtst <u>hehr</u>·kohm·uhn
I need an English-speaking doctor.	**Ich brauche einen englischsprechenden Arzt.** eekh <u>browkh</u>·uh <u>ien</u>·uhn <u>ehng</u>·gleesh·shprehkh·ehnd·uhn ahrtst
What are the office hours?	**Wann sind die Sprechstunden?** vahn zihnt dee <u>shprekh</u>·shtoond·uhn
I'd like an appointment for...	**Ich möchte einen Termin für ...** eekh <u>merkht</u>·uh <u>ien</u>·uhn tehr·<u>meen</u> fewr ...
– today	**– heute** <u>hoy</u>·tuh
– tomorrow	**– morgen** <u>mohr</u>·guhn
– as soon as possible	**– so bald wie möglich** zoh bahld vee <u>merg</u>·leekh
It's urgent.	**Es ist dringend.** ehs ihst <u>dreeng</u>·uhnt

Symptoms

I'm bleeding.	**Ich blute.** eekh <u>bloot</u>·uh
I'm constipated.	**Ich habe Verstopfung.** eekh <u>hahb</u>·uh fehr·<u>shtohpf</u>·oong
I'm dizzy.	**Mir ist schwindlig.** meer ihst <u>shvihnd</u>·leek
I'm nauseous.	**Mir ist schlecht.** meer ihst shlehkht
I'm vomiting.	**Ich übergebe mich.** eekh ewb·ehr·<u>gehb</u>·uh meekh
It hurts here.	**Es tut hier weh.** ehs toot heer veh
I have…	**Ich habe …** eekh <u>hahb</u>·uh …
– an allergic reaction	**– eine allergische Reaktion** <u>ien</u>·uh ah·<u>lehr</u>·geesh·uh reh·ahk·<u>syon</u>
– chest pain	**– Brustschmerzen** <u>broost</u>·shmehrt·suhn
– cramps	**– Krämpfe** <u>krehmp</u>·fuh
– diarrhea	**– Durchfall** <u>doorkh</u>·fahl
– an earache	**– Ohrenschmerzen** <u>oht</u>·uhn·shmehrt·suhn
– a fever	**– Fieber** <u>feeb</u>·ehr
– pain	**– Schmerzen** <u>shmehrt</u>·suhn
– a rash	**– einen Ausschlag** <u>ien</u>·uhn <u>ows</u>·shlahg
– a sprain	**– eine Verstauchung** <u>ien</u>·uh fehr·<u>shtowkh</u>·oong
– some swelling	**– eine Schwellung** <u>ien</u>·uh <u>shvehl</u>·oong
– a sore throat	**– Halsschmerzen** <u>hahls</u>·shmehrt·suhn
– a stomachache	**– Magenschmerzen** <u>mahg</u>·uhn·shmehrt·suhn
– sunstroke	**– einen Sonnenstich** <u>ien</u>·uhn <u>zohn</u>·uhn·shteekh
I've been sick [ill] for…days.	**Ich bin seit … Tagen krank.** eekh bihn ziet … <u>tahg</u>·uhn krahnk

▶ For numbers, see page 167.

Health Conditions

I'm...	**Ich bin ...** eekh bihn ...
– anemic	– **anämisch** ah·<u>nay</u>·meesh
– asthmatic	– **Asthmatiker** ahst·<u>maht</u>·eek·ehr
– diabetic	– **Diabetiker** dee·ah·<u>beht</u>·eek·ehr
I'm allergic to *antibiotics/penicillin*.	**Ich bin allergisch auf** *Antibiotika/ Penicillin*. eekh bihn <u>ah</u>·lehrg·eesh owf *ahn·tee·bee·oh·tee·kah/peh·nih·<u>sihl</u>·ihn*

▶ For food items, see page 84.

I have...	**Ich habe ...** eekh <u>hahb</u>·uh ...
– arthritis	– **Arthritis** <u>ahr</u>·tree·tihs
– a heart condition	– **eine Herzkrankheit** <u>ien</u>·uh <u>hehrts</u>·krahnk·hiet
– *high/low* blood pressure	– *hohen/niedrigen* **Blutdruck** <u>hoh</u>·uhn/ <u>need</u>·ree·gehn <u>bloot</u>·drook
I'm on...	**Ich nehme ...** eekh <u>nehm</u>·uh ...

You May Hear...

Was stimmt nicht mit Ihnen? vahs shtihmt neekht miht <u>eehn</u>·uhn	What's wrong?
Wo tut es weh? voh toot ehs veh	Where does it hurt?
Tut es hier weh? toot ehs heer veh	Does it hurt here?
Nehmen Sie Medikamente? <u>nehm</u>·uhn zee mehd·ee·kah·<u>mehnt</u>·uh	Are you on medication?
Sind Sie auf irgendetwas allergisch? zihnt zee owf eer·guhnd·<u>eht</u>·vahs ah·<u>lehr</u>·geesh	Are you allergic to anything?
Öffnen Sie Ihren Mund. <u>erf</u>·nuhn zee <u>eehr</u>·uhn moont	Open your mouth.
Tief einatmen. teef ien·<u>aht</u>·muhn	Breathe deeply.

Bitte husten. biht·tuh hoos·tuhn	Cough, please.
Gehen Sie ins Krankenhaus. geh·uhn zee ihns krahnk·uhn·hows	Go to the hospital.
Es ist ... ehs ihst ...	It's...
– **gebrochen** geh·brohkh·uhn	– broken
– **ansteckend** ahn·shtehk·uhnt	– contagious
– **infiziert** een·fee·tseert	– infected
– **verstaucht** fehr·shtowkht	– sprained
– **nichts Ernstes** neekhts ehrnst·uhs	– nothing serious

Treatment

Do I need *a prescription/ medicine*?	**Brauche ich *ein Rezept/Medikament*?** browkh·uh eekh ien reh·tsehpt/mehd·ee·kah·mehnt
Can you prescribe a generic drug?	**Können Sie ein ähnliches, günstiges Medikament verschreiben?** kern·uhn zee ien ehn·lee·khehs gewn·stee·guhs meh·dee·kah·mehnt fehr·shrieb·uhn
Where can I get it?	**Wo kann ich es bekommen?** voh kahn eekh ehs buh·kohm·uhn
Is this over the counter?	**Ist es rezeptfrei?** ihst ehs reh·tsehpt·frie

▶ For dosage instructions, see page 158.

Hospital

Notify my family, please.	**Bitte benachrichtigen Sie meine Familie.** biht·tuh buh·nahkh·reekh·tih·guhn zee mien·uh fah·mee·lee·uh
I'm in pain.	**Ich habe Schmerzen.** eekh hahb·uh shmehrt·suhn
I need a *doctor/nurse*.	**Ich brauche *einen Arzt/eine Schwester*.** eekh browkh·uh ien·uhn ahrtst/ien·uh shvehs·tehr

| When are visiting hours? | **Wann ist die Besuchszeit?** vahn ihst dee beh-<u>zookhs</u>-tsiet |
| I'm visiting... | **Ich besuche ...** eekh beh-<u>zookh</u>-uh ... |

Dentist

I have...	**Ich habe ...** eekh <u>hahb</u>-uh ...
– a broken tooth	**– einen kaputten Zahn** <u>ien</u>-uhn kah-<u>poot</u>-uhn tsahn
– a lost filling	**– eine Füllung verloren** <u>ien</u>-uh <u>fewl</u>-oong fehr-<u>lohr</u>-uhn
– a toothache	**– Zahnschmerzen** <u>tsahn</u>-shmehrts-uhn
Can you fix this denture?	**Können Sie diese Prothese reparieren?** <u>kern</u>-uhn zee <u>deez</u>-uh proh-<u>teh</u>-zuh reh-pah-<u>reer</u>-uhn

Gynecologist

I have *cramps/ a vaginal infection*.	**Ich habe *Krämpfe/eine Scheideninfektion*.** eekh <u>hahb</u>-uh *<u>krehmp</u>-fuh/<u>ie</u>-nuh <u>shnied</u>-uhn-ihn-fehk-tyohn*
I missed my period.	**Meine Periode ist ausgeblieben.** <u>mien</u>-uh pehr-<u>yoh</u>-duh ihst <u>ows</u>-geh-bleeb-uhn
I'm on the Pill.	**Ich nehme die Pille.** eekh <u>nehm</u>-uh dee pihl-uh
I'm (not) pregnant.	**Ich bin (nicht) schwanger.** eekh bihn (neekht) <u>shvahng</u>-ehr
My last period was...	**Meine letzte Periode war ...** <u>mien</u>-uh <u>lehts</u>-uh pehr-<u>yohd</u>-uh vahr ...

Optician

I lost...	**Ich habe ... verloren.** eekh <u>hahb</u>-uh ... fehr-<u>lohr</u>-uhn
– a contact lens	**– eine Kontaktlinse** <u>ien</u>-uh <u>kohn</u>-tahkt-lihnz-uh
– my glasses	**– meine Brille** <u>mien</u>-uh <u>brihl</u>-uh
– a lens	**– ein Brillenglas** ien <u>brihl</u>-uhn-glahs

Payment and Insurance

How much?	**Wie viel kostet es?** vee feel <u>kohs</u>·tuht ehs
Can I pay by credit card?	**Kann ich mit Kreditkarte bezahlen?** kahn eekh miht kreh·<u>deet</u>·kahr·tuh beht·<u>sahl</u>·uhn
I have insurance.	**Ich bin versichert.** eekh bihn fehr·<u>zeekh</u>·ehrt
I need a receipt for my insurance.	**Ich brauche eine Quittung für meine Versicherung.** eekh <u>browkh</u>·uh <u>ien</u>·uh <u>kviht</u>·oong fewr <u>mien</u>·uh fehr·<u>zeekh</u>·ehr·oong

Pharmacy [Chemist]

Essential

Where's the pharmacy [chemist]?	**Wo ist die Apotheke?** voh ihst dee ah·poh·<u>tehk</u>·uh
What time does it *open/close*?	**Wann *öffnet/schließt* sie?** vahn *<u>erf</u>·nuht/ shleest* zee
What would you recommend for…?	**Was empfehlen Sie bei …?** vahs ehm·<u>pfeh</u>·luhn zee bie …
How much do I take?	**Wie viel muss ich einnehmen?** vee feel moos eekh <u>nehm</u>·uhn
Can you fill [make up] this prescription?	**Können Sie mir die Medikamente für dieses Rezept geben?** <u>kern</u>·uhn zee meer dee meh·dee·kah·<u>mehnt</u>·uh fewr <u>deez</u>·uhs reht·<u>sehpt</u> <u>geh</u>·buhn
I'm allergic to…	**Ich bin allergisch auf …** eekh bihn ah·<u>lehr</u>·gihsh owf …

i In Germany, there is a distinction between **Apotheke** (pharmacy) and **Drogerie** (drugstore).
Die Apotheke, usually featuring a large red A sign 🜪 , dispenses prescription and over-the-counter medication.
Die Drogerie sells toiletries and other personal items. Pharmacies are open 9:00 a.m. to 6:30 p.m. Monday through Friday, and from 9:00 a.m. to 1:00 p.m. (sometimes 4:00 p.m) on Saturday. Most large cities and towns have at least one 24-hour pharmacy. Closed pharmacies will have a sign on the door indicating the nearest 24-hour location.

Dosage Instructions

How much do I take?	**Wie viel muss ich einnehmen?** vee feel moos eekh <u>ien</u>·nehm·uhn
How often?	**Wie oft?** vee ohft
Is it safe for children?	**Ist es für Kinder geeignet?** ihst ehs fewr <u>kihnd</u>·ehr geh·<u>ieg</u>·nuht
I'm taking…	**Ich nehme …** eekh <u>neh</u>·muh …
Are there side effects?	**Gibt es Nebenwirkungen?** gihpt ehs <u>nehb</u>·uhn·veerk·oong·uhn

You May See...

EINMAL/DREIMAL **AM TAG**	*once/three* times a day
TABLETTE	tablet
TROPFEN	drop
TEELÖFFEL	teaspoon
NACH/VOR/MIT **DEN MAHLZEITEN**	*after/before/with* meals
AUF LEEREN MAGEN	on an empty stomach
IM GANZEN SCHLUCKEN	swallow whole
KANN BENOMMENHEIT VERURSACHEN	may cause drowsiness
NUR ZÜR ÄUSSEREN ANWENDUNG	for external use only

Health Problems

I need something for...	**Ich brauche etwas gegen ...** ihkh <u>browkh</u>·uh <u>eht</u>·vahs <u>geh</u>·guhn ...
– a cold	– **eine Erkältung** <u>ien</u>·uh ehr·<u>kehlt</u>·oong
– a cough	– **Husten** <u>hoos</u>·tuhn
– diarrhea	– **Durchfall** <u>doorkh</u>·fahl
– insect bites	– **Insektenstiche** een·<u>zehkt</u>·uhn·shteekh·uh
– motion [travel] sickness	– **die Reisekrankheit** <u>riez</u>·uh·krahnk·hiet
– a sore throat	– **Halsschmerzen** <u>hahls</u>·shmehrt·suhn
– sunburn	– **Sonnenbrand** <u>zohn</u>·uhn·brahnt
– an upset stomach	– **eine Magenverstimmung** <u>ien</u>·uh <u>mahg</u>·uhn·fehr·shtihm·oong

Basic Needs

I'd like...	**Ich hätte gern ...** eekh <u>heh</u>·tuh gehrn ...
– acetaminophen [paracetamol]	– **Paracetamol** pah·rah·<u>seht</u>·ah·mohl
– antiseptic cream	– **eine antiseptische Creme** ahn·tee·<u>zehp</u>·tee·shuh krehm
– aspirin	– **Aspirin** ahs·pih·<u>reen</u>
– bandages	– **Pflaster** <u>pflahs</u>·tehr
– a comb	– **einen Kamm** <u>ien</u>·uhn kahm
– condoms	– **Kondome** kohn·<u>dohm</u>·uh
– contact lens solution	– **Kontaktlinsenlösung** kohn·<u>tahkt</u>·lehnz·uhn·lerz·oong
– deodorant	– **Deodorant** deh·oh·doh·<u>rahnt</u>
– a hairbrush	– **eine Haarbürste** <u>ien</u>·uh hahr·bewr·stuh
– hairspray	– **Haarspray** <u>hahr</u>·shpraye
– ibuprofen	– **Ibuprofen** ee·boo·proh·<u>fuhn</u>
– insect repellent	– **Insektenspray** ihn·<u>zehkt</u>·uhn·shpray
– lotion	– **Lotion** loht·<u>syohn</u>
– a nail file	– **eine Nagelfeile** <u>ien</u>·uh <u>nahg</u>·ehl·fie·luh
– a (disposable) razor	– **(Wegwerf-) Rasierer** <u>vehk</u>·vehrf rah·<u>zeer</u>·ehr
– razor blades	– **Rasierklingen** rah·<u>zeer</u>·kleeng·uhn
– rubbing alcohol [surgical spirit]	– **Franzbranntwein** <u>frahnts</u>·brahnt·vien
– sanitary napkins [pads]	– **Monatsbinden** <u>moh</u>·nahts·bihnd·uhn
– shampoo/ conditioner	– **Shampoo/Spülung** <u>shahm</u>·poo/<u>shpewl</u>·oong
– soap	– **Seife** <u>zie</u>·fuh
– sunscreen	– **Sonnenmilch** <u>zohn</u>·nuhn·mihlkh

– tampons	– **Tampons** <u>tahm</u>·pohns	
– tissues	– **Taschentücher** <u>tahsh</u>·uhn·tewkh·ehr	
– toilet paper	– **Toilettenpapier** toy·<u>leht</u>·uhn·pah·peer	
– toothpaste	– **Zahnpasta** <u>tsahn</u>·pahs·tah	

▶For baby products, see page 144.

Reference

Grammar

Regular Verbs and Their Tenses

Regular verbs in German are conjugated as in the table below. Note that the past is expressed with **haben** (to have) or **sein** (to be) plus the past participle. The future is formed with **werden** (will) plus the infinitive.

BEZAHLEN (to pay)		Present	Past	Future
I	**ich**	bezahl**e**	habc bezahlt	werde bezahlen
you (inf.)	**du**	bezahl**st**	hast bezahlt	wirst bezahlen
he/she/it	**er/sie/es**	bezahl**t**	hat bezahlt	wird bezahlen
we	**wir**	bezahl**en**	haben bezahlt	werden bezahlen
you (pl.) (inf.)	**ihr**	bezahl**t**	habt bezahlt	werdet bezahlen
they/you	**sle/Sie**	bezahl**en**	haben bezahlt	werden bezahlen

Example: **Ich bezahle bar.** I'll pay in cash.
Er♂/sie♀ bezahlt mit Kreditkarte. He/She will pay with credit card.

MACHEN (to do, make)		Present	Past	Future
I	**ich**	mach**e**	habe gemacht	werde machen
you (inf.)	**du**	mach**st**	hast gemacht	wirst machen
he/she/it	**er/sie/es**	mach**t**	hat gemacht	wird machen
we	**wir**	mach**en**	haben gemacht	werden machen
you (pl.) (inf.)	**ihr**	mach**t**	habt gemacht	werdet machen
they/you	**sie/Sie**	mach**en**	haben gemacht	werden machen

Examples: **Ich mache hier Urlaub.** I'm here on vacation.
Was machen Sie beruflich? What do you do (for work)?

Irregular Verbs

There are a number of irregular verbs in German. Two common irregular verbs in German are **haben** (to have) and **sein** (to be). Conjugations follow:

HABEN (to have)		Present	Past	Future
I	**ich**	habe	habe gehabt	werde haben
you (inf.)	**du**	hast	hast gehabt	wirst haben
he/she/it	**er/sie/es**	hat	hat gehabt	wird haben
we	**wir**	haben	haben gehabt	werden haben
you (pl.) (inf.)	**ihr**	habt	habt gehabt	werdet haben
they/you	**sie/Sie**	haben	haben gehabt	werden haben

Example: **Ich habe einen Koffer.** I have one suitcase.
Ihr habt viel zu tun. You guys have a lot to do.

SEIN (to be)		Present	Past	Future
I	**ich**	bin	bin gewesen	werde sein
you (inf.)	**du**	bist	bist gewesen	wirst sein
he/she/it	**er/sie/es**	ist	ist gewesen	wird sein
we	**wir**	sind	sind gewesen	werden sein
you (pl.) (inf.)	**ihr**	seid	seid gewesen	werdet sein
they/you	**sie/Sie**	sind	sind gewesen	werden sein

Example: **Ich bin geschäftlich hier.** I am here on business.
Wir sind glücklich. We are happy.

Nouns and Articles

In German, all nouns are capitalized. German nouns are also gender-specific; they can be masculine, feminine or neuter. There is no easy way to determine whether a noun is masculine, feminine or neuter.

There are three definite articles (the) in German: **der**, **die** and **das**. Masculine words use **der**, feminine words use **die** and neuter words use **das**. The only way to tell whether a word is masculine, feminine or neuter is to look at the article. For this reason, it is best to memorize the article when learning the word. For plural nouns using a definite article, all genders use **die**.

Definite examples: **der Mann** (the man), **die Männer** (the men); **die Frau** (the woman), **die Frauen** (the women); **das Kind** (neuter) (the child), **die Kinder** (neuter) (the children)

There are four cases in German. The definite articles are as follows:

	masculine	feminine	neuter	plural (all genders)
nominative	**der**	**die**	**das**	**die**
accusative	**den**	**die**	**das**	**die**
dative	**dem**	**der**	**dem**	**den**
genitive	**des**	**der**	**des**	**der**

German uses two indefinite articles (a/an): **ein** and **eine**. Masculine and neuter nouns use **ein**, and feminine nouns use **eine**. For plural nouns, the indefinite article is dropped, as in English.

Indefinite examples: **ein Zug** (a train), **Züge** (trains); **eine Karte** (a map), **Karten** (maps)

Word Order

German is similar to English in terms of word order for simple sentences; it follows the subject-verb-object pattern.

Example: **Wir lassen unser Gepäck hier.** We leave our luggage here.

When the sentence doesn't begin with a subject, the word order changes: the verb and the subject are inverted.

Examples:

	Er	**ist**	**in Berlin**		He is in Berlin.
Heute	**ist**	**er**	**in Berlin**		Today he is in Berlin.
	Wir	**sind**	**in Berlin**	**gewesen.**	We were in Berlin.

To ask a question, begin with the verb and follow with the subject, as in English. Example: **Seid ihr in Köln gewesen?** Have you been to Cologne? (Literally: Have you to Cologne been?)

Negation

The negative is formed by putting **nicht** after the verb.

Example: **Ich bin Thomas.** I am Thomas.
Ich bin nicht Thomas. I am not Thomas.

If a noun is used, the negation is made by adding **kein** (masculine and neuter), or **keine** (feminine). For plural nouns, always add **keine**.

Example: **Wir haben keine Einzelzimmer**. We don't have any single rooms.

Imperatives

Whereas in English the imperative always looks like the infinitive ("Go!"), in German it is derived from the **du-/Sie-** form of the present tense. In the **du-** form, the **-st** is dropped. All other forms are identical to the present tense. The verb always comes first in commands.

		Go!
du	you (inf.)	**Geh!**
ihr	you (pl.) (inf.)	**Geht!**
Sie	you	**Gehen Sie!**
wir	we	**Gehen wir!** (Let's go!)

Comparative and Superlative

In German, the comparative of an adjective is usually formed by adding **–er** to the end of the adjective.

Examples: **klein** (small), **kleiner** (smaller); **billig** (cheap), **billiger** (cheaper); **groß** (big), **größer** (bigger)

The superlative is formed by adding **–sten** or **–esten** to the end of the adjective. If the adjective has a vowel of **a**, **o** or **u**, it may change to **ä**, **ö** or **ü** in the comparative and superlative forms.

Examples: **klein** (small), **kleinsten** (smallest); **billig** (cheap), **billigsten** (cheapest); **groß** (big); **größten** (biggest)

Possessive Pronouns

Possessive pronouns agree in gender and number with the noun they replace.

	Masculine	Feminine	Neuter
mine	**meiner**	**meine**	**meines**
yours (inf.)	**deiner**	**deine**	**deines**
his/its	**seiner**	**seine**	**seines**
hers/theirs	**ihrer**	**ihre**	**ihres**
ours	**unserer**	**unsere**	**unseres**
yours (pl.) (inf.)	**eurer**	**eure**	**eures**

Example: **Wem gehört der Schlüssel?** Whose key is this? **Das ist meiner.** It's mine.

Adjectives

Adjectives must agree with the nouns they modify. Adjective endings change based on the article used and the case. For masculine nouns, **–er** is added to the adjective after an indefinite article and **–e** is added after a definite article.

Example: **ein klein*er* Herr** a short gentleman
der klein*e* Herr the short gentleman

For feminine nouns, **–e** is added to the adjective after both an indefinite and a definite article.

Example: **eine kluge Frau** an intelligent woman
die kluge Frau the intelligent woman

For neuter nouns, **–es** is added to the adjective after an indefinite article, while **–e** is added to the adjective after a definite article.

Example: **ein gro<u>ßes</u> Land** a big country
das gro<u>ße</u> Land the big country

Possessive adjectives must agree in gender and number with the noun they are associated with.

	singular		plural
	masculine/neuter	feminine	
my	**mein**	**meine**	**meine**
your (inf.)	**dein**	**deine**	**deine**
his/its	**sein**	**seine**	**seine**
her/their	**ihr**	**ihre**	**ihre**
your (pl.) (inf.)	**Ihr**	**Ihre**	**Ihre**
our	**unser**	**unsere**	**unsere**

Example: **Wir lassen unser Gepäck im Hotel.** We leave our luggage in the hotel.

Adverbs and Adverbial Expressions

In German, adverbs are usually identical to adjectives but, unlike adjectives, their endings don't change.

Examples:

Adjective: **das <u>gute</u> Essen** the good food

Adverb: **Sie sprechen <u>gut</u> Deutsch.** You speak German well.

Numbers

Essential

0	**null**	nool
1	**eins**	iens
2	**zwei**	tsvie
3	**drei**	drie
4	**vier**	feer
5	**fünf**	fewnf
6	**sechs**	zehks
7	**sieben**	<u>zeeb</u>·uhn
8	**acht**	ahkht
9	**neun**	noyn
10	**zehn**	tsehn
11	**elf**	ehlf
12	**zwölf**	tsverlf
13	**dreizehn**	<u>drie</u>·tsehn
14	**vierzehn**	<u>feert</u>·tsehn
15	**fünfzehn**	<u>fewnf</u>·tsehn
16	**sechszehn**	<u>zehk</u>·tsehn
17	**siebzehn**	<u>zeep</u>·tsehn
18	**achtzehn**	<u>ahkht</u>·tsehn
19	**neunzehn**	<u>noyn</u>·tsehn
20	**zwanzig**	<u>tsvahnt</u>·seek
21	**einundzwanzig**	<u>ien</u>·oond·tsvahn·tseek
22	**zweiundzwanzig**	<u>tsvie</u>·oond·tsvahn·tseek
30	**dreißig**	<u>drie</u>·seekh

31	**einunddreißig** ien·oont·drie·seekh
40	**vierzig** feert·seek
50	**fünfzig** fewnf·tseeg
60	**sechzig** zehkht·seeg
70	**siebzig** zeeb·tseeg
80	**achtzig** ahkht·tseeg
90	**neunzig** noynt·seek
100	**einhundert** ien·hoon·dehrt
101	**einhunderteins** ien·hoon·dehr·tiens
200	**zweihundert** tsvie·hoon·dehrt
500	**fünfhundert** fewnf·hoon·dehrt
1,000	**eintausend** ien·tow·zuhnt
10,000	**zehntausend** tsehn·tow·zuhnt
1,000,000	**eine Million** ien·uh mihl·yohn

Ordinal Numbers

first	**erste** ehrs·tuh
second	**zweite** tsviet·uh
third	**dritte** driht·tuh
fourth	**vierte** feer·tuh
fifth	**fünfte** fewnf·tuh
once	**einmal** ien·mahl
twice	**zweimal** tsvie·mahl
three times	**dreimal** drie·mahl

Essential

What time is it?	**Wie spät ist es?** vee shpayt ihst ehs
It's noon [midday].	**Es ist zwölf.** ehs ihst tsverlf
At midnight.	**Um Mitternacht.** oom miht·tehr·nahkht
From one o'clock to two o'clock.	**Von eins bis zwei.** fohn iens bihs tsvie
Five after [past] three.	**Fünf nach drei.** fewnf nahkh drie
A quarter to four.	**Viertel vor vier.** feert·uhl fohr feer
5:30 a.m./5:30 p.m.	**Fünf Uhr dreißig/Siebzehn Uhr dreißig** fewnf oohr drie·seeg/zeeb·tsuhn oohr drie·seeg

Germans use the 24-hour clock in formal contexts (radio, TV, transportation schedules and digital clocks) or when confusion might otherwise arise. The morning hours from 1:00 a.m. to noon are the same as in English. After that, just add 12 to the time: 1:00 p.m. would be 13:00, 5:00 p.m. would be 17:00 and so on. This system eliminates the necessity of "a.m." and "p.m." markers. When the 12-hour clock is used, **morgens** (in the morning) and **abends** (in the evening) are added after the number for clarity.

Days

Monday	**Montag** <u>mohn</u>·tahk
Tuesday	**Dienstag** <u>deens</u>·tahk
Wednesday	**Mittwoch** <u>miht</u>·vohkh
Thursday	**Donnerstag** <u>dohn</u>·ehrs·tahk
Friday	**Freitag** <u>frie</u>·tahk
Saturday	**Samstag** <u>zahms</u>·tahk
Sunday	**Sonntag** <u>zohn</u>·tahk

 German calendars and weeks, like the U.K., are arranged Monday through Sunday (in contrast to the U.S., where calendars run Sunday through Saturday).

Dates

yesterday	**gestern** <u>gehs</u>·tehrn
today	**heute** <u>hoy</u>·tuh
tomorrow	**morgen** <u>mohr</u>·guhn
day	**Tag** tahk
week	**Woche** <u>vohkh</u>·uh
month	**Monat** <u>moh</u>·naht
year	**Jahr** yahr

Months

January	**Januar** <u>yahn</u>·wahr
February	**Februar** <u>fehb</u>·rooahr
March	**März** mehrts
April	**April** ah·<u>prihl</u>
May	**Mai** mie
June	**Juni** <u>yoo</u>·nee
July	**Juli** <u>yoo</u>·lee
August	**August** <u>ow</u>·goost
September	**September** zehp·<u>tehm</u>·behr
October	**Oktober** ohk·<u>toh</u>·behr
November	**November** noh·<u>vehm</u>·behr
December	**Dezember** deh·<u>tsehm</u>·behr

Seasons

in...	**im ...** ihm ...
– spring	**– Frühling** <u>frewh</u>·leeng
– summer	**– Sommer** <u>zohm</u>·ehr
– fall [autumn]	**– Herbst** hehrbst
– winter	**– Winter** <u>vihnt</u>·ehr

Holidays

January 1: New Year's Day, **Neujahrstag**

January 6: Epiphany, **Heilige Drei Könige**

May 1: Labor Day, **Tag der Arbeit**

August 15: Assumption Day, **Mariä Himmelfahrt**

October 3: German Unity Day, **Tag der Deutschen Einheit**

November 1: All Saint's Day, **Allerheiligen**

December 25: Christmas, **Erster Weihnachtstag**

December 26: St. Stephen's Day [Boxing Day], **Zweiter Weihnachtstag**

The Easter (movable) holidays are:

Ascension Day, **Christ Himmelfahrt**

Easter Sunday, **Ostersonntag**

Easter Monday, **Ostermontag**

Feast of Corpus Christi, **Fronleichnam**

Good Friday, **Karfreitag**

Pentecost, **Pfinstsonntag**

Pentecost Monday, **Pfinstmontag**

i One of Germany's most famous festivals is **Oktoberfest**, held each September in Munich. This food and beer festival extends for more than two weeks and is attended by about six million visitors from around the world. Another popular festival is **Karneval**, celebrated with parades and parties the week before Lent in areas that have substantial Catholic populations. Christmas festivities and markets are also very popular in Germany. Locals and tourists alike visit these markets to purchase local handmade crafts such as toys, wooden carvings, marionettes, candles, lambskin shoes and much more. There are plenty of food vendors available with numerous tasty treats to try.

Conversion Tables

When you know	Multiply by	To find
ounces	28.3	grams
pounds	0.45	kilograms
inches	2.54	centimeters
feet	0.3	meters
miles	1.61	kilometers
square inches	6.45	sq. centimeters
square feet	0.09	sq. meters
square miles	2.59	sq. kilometers
pints (U.S./Brit)	0.47/0.56	liters
gallons (U.S./Brit)	3.8/4.5	liters
Fahrenheit	5/9, after −32	Centigrade
Centigrade	9/5, then +32	Fahrenheit

Measurement

1 gram	**ein Gramm** ien grahm	= 0.035 oz.
1 kilogram (kg)	**ein Kilogramm** ien <u>kee</u>·loh·grahm	= 2.2 lb
1 liter (l)	**ein Liter** ien <u>lee</u>·tehr	= 1.06 U.S/0.88 Brit. quarts
1 centimeter (cm)	**ein Zentimeter** ien <u>tsehn</u>·tee·muh·tehr	= 0.4 inch
1 meter (m)	**ein Meter** ien <u>meh</u>·tehr	= 39.37 inches/3.28 ft.
1 kilometer (km)	**ein Kilometer** ien <u>kee</u>·loh·meh·tehr	= 0.62 mile

Mileage

1 km – 0.62 mi	20 km – 12.4 mi
5 km – 3.10 mi	50 km – 31.0 mi
10 km – 6.20 mi	100 km – 61.0 mi

Temperature

-40° C – -40° F	-1° C – 30° F	20° C – 68° F
-30° C – -22° F	0° C – 32° F	25° C – 77° F
-20° C – -4° F	5° C – 41° F	30° C – 86° F
-10° C – 14° F	10° C – 50° F	35° C – 95° F
-5° C – 23° F	15° C – 59° F	

Oven Temperature

100° C – 212° F	175° C – 347° F	204° C – 400° F
121° C – 250° F	177° C – 350° F	220° C – 428° F
149° C – 300° F	180° C – 356° F	250° C – 482° F
150° C – 302° F	200° C – 392° F	260° C – 500° F

Related Websites

www.tsa.gov
U.S. Transportation Security Administration (TSA)

www.caa.co.uk
U.K. Civil Aviation Authority (CAA)

www.lufthansa.com
Lufthansa (national airline of Germany) website

www.bahn.de, www.raileurope.com, www.der.com
Train information websites

www.bedandbreakfast.de
German bed and breakfast website

www.landtourismus.de
German agritourism website

www.jugendherberge.de
Youth hostels website

www.hihostels.com
Hostelling International website

www.post.de
Germany's post office website

www.germany-tourism.de
National German tourist board information website

English–German Dictionary

A

accept *v* akzeptieren
access *n* der Zutritt
accident der Unfall
accommodation die Unterkunft
account *n* **(bank)** das Konto
acupuncture die Akupunktur
adapter der Adapter
address *n* die Adresse
admission (price) der Eintritt
after nach;
  ~noon der Nachmittag;
  ~shave das Aftershave
age *n* das Alter
agency die Agentur
AIDS AIDS
air *n* die Luft; **~ conditioning**
  die Klimaanlage; **~-dry**
  lufttrocknen; **~ pump**
  die Luftpumpe; **~line**
  die Fluggesellschaft; **~mail**
  die Luftpost; **~plane** das
  Flugzeug; **~port** der Flughafen
aisle der Gang; **~ seat** der
  Platz am Gang
allergic allergisch; **~ reaction**
  die allergische Reaktion

allow erlauben
alone allein
alter *v* umändern
alternate route die
  Alternativroute
aluminum foil die
  Aluminiumfolie
amazing erstaunlich
ambulance der Krankenwagen
American *adj* amerikanisch
amusement park der
  Vergnügungspark
anemic anämisch
anesthesia die Anästhesie
animal das Tier
ankle das Fußgelenk
antibiotic *n* das Antibiotikum
antiques store das
  Antiquitätengeschäft
antiseptic cream die
  antiseptische Creme
apartment das Apartment
appendix (body part) der
  Blinddarm
appetizer die Vorspeise
appointment der Termin
arcade die Spielhalle
area code die Ortsvorwahl
arm *n* **(body part)** der Arm
aromatherapy die
  Aromatherapie
around (the corner) um;
  ~ (price) ungefähr

adj	adjective	BE	British English	*prep*	preposition
adv	adverb	*n*	noun	*v*	verb

arrival Ankunft
arrive ankommen
artery die Arterie
arthritis die Arthritis
art die Kunst
Asian *adj* asiatisch
aspirin das Aspirin
asthmatic asthmatisch
ATM der Bankautomat;
~ **card** die Bankkarte
attack *v* angreifen
attraction (place) die
Sehenswürdigkeit
attractive attraktiv
Australia das Australien
Australian *adj* australisch
automatic automatisch;
~ **car** das Auto mit
Automatikschaltung
available verfügbar

B

baby das Baby;
~ **bottle** die Babyflasche;
~ **wipe** das Baby-Pflegetuch;
~**sitter** der Babysitter
back (body part) der Rücken;
~**ache** die Rückenschmerzen;
~**pack** der Rucksack
bag die Tasche
baggage [BE] das Gepäck;
~ **claim** die Gepäckausgabe;
~ **ticket** der Gepäckschein
bake *v* backen
bakery die Bäckerei

ballet das Ballett
bandage das Pflaster
bank *n* die Bank
bar (place) die Bar
barbecue (device) *n* der Grill
barber der Herrenfriseur
baseball der Baseball
basket (grocery store)
der Einkaufskorb
basketball der Basketball
bathroom das Bad
battery die Batterie
battleground das
Schlachtfeld
be *v* sein
beach der Strand
beautiful wunderschön;
~ schön
bed *n* das Bett; ~ **and**
breakfast
die Pension
before vor
begin beginnen
beginner der Anfänger
behind (direction) hinter
beige *adj* beige
belt der Gürtel
best *adj* beste; ~ **before**
mindestens haltbar bis
better besser
bicycle das Fahrrad
big groß; ~**ger** größerger
bike route die Radroute
bikini der Bikini
bill *n* **(money)** der Geldschein;
~ *n* **(of sale)** die Rechnung

bird der Vogel
birthday der Geburtstag
black *adj* schwarz
bladder die Blase
bland fad
blanket die Decke
bleed bluten
blender der Mixer
blood das Blut; **~ pressure**
der Blutdruck
blouse die Bluse
blue *adj* blau
board *v* einsteigen;
~ing pass die Bordkarte
boat *n* das Boot
boil *v* kochen
bone *n* der Knochen
book *n* das Buch;
~store der Buchladen
boot *n* der Stiefel
boring langweilig
botanical garden
der botanische Garten
bother *v* belästigen
bottle *n* die Flasche;
~ opener der Flaschenöffner
bowl *n* die Schüssel
boxing match der
Boxkampf
boy der Junge;
~friend der Freund
bra der BH
bracelet das Armband
brake (car) die Bremse
breaded paniert
break *v* **(bone)** brechen

breakdown (car) die Panne
breakfast *n* das Frühstück
break-in (burglary) *n* der
Einbruch
breast die Brust;
~feed *v* stillen
breathe atmen
bridge die Brücke
briefs (clothing) der
Schlüpfer
bring bringen
British *adj* britisch
broken kaputt; **~ (bone)**
gebrochen
brooch die Brosche
broom der Besen
brother der Bruder
brown *adj* braun
bug (insect) *n* das Insekt
building das Gebäude
burn *v* brennen
bus *n* der Bus;
~ station der Busbahnhof;
~ stop die Bushaltestelle;
~ ticket die Busfahrkarte;
~ tour die Busreise
business *adj* Geschäfts-;
~ card die Visitenkarte;
~ center das
Geschäftszentrum;
~ class die Business-Class;
~ hours die Öffnungszeiten
butcher *n* der Fleischer
buttocks der Po
buy *v* kaufen
bye auf Wiedersehen

cabaret das Kabarett
cable car die Seilbahn
cafe (place) das Café
call v **(phone)** anrufen;
~ n der Anruf ~ **collect** ein
R-Gespräch führen
calorie die Kalorie
camera die Kamera;
~ **case** die Kameratasche;
digital ~ die Digitalkamera
camp v campen; ~**ing stove**
der Campingkocher;
~**site** der Campingplatz
can opener der Dosenöffner
Canada das Kanada
Canadian adj kanadisch
cancel stornieren
candy die Süßigkeit
canned good die Konserve
canyon der Canyon
car das Auto;
~ **hire [BE]** die Autovermietung;
~ **park [BE]** der Parkplatz;
~ **rental** die Autovermietung;
~ **seat** der Autositz
carafe die Karaffe
card n die Karte;
ATM ~ die Bankkarte;
credit ~ die Kreditkarte;
debit ~ die EC-Karte;
phone ~ die Telefonkarte
carry-on n **(piece of hand
luggage)** das
Handgepäckstück

cart (grocery store) der
Einkaufswagen; ~ **(luggage)**
der Gepäckwagen
carton (of cigarettes)
die Stange (Zigaretten);
~ **(of groceries)** die
Packung
cash n das Bargeld;
~ v einlösen
cashier der Kassierer
casino das Casino
castle das Schloss
cathedral die Kathedrale
cave n die Höhle
CD die CD
cell phone das Handy
Celsius Celsius
centimeter der Zentimeter
certificate das Zertifikat
chair n der Stuhl;
~ **lift** der Sessellift
change v **(baby)** wickeln;
~ **(buses)** umsteigen;
~ **(money)** wechseln;
~ n **(money)** das
Wechselgeld
charge v **(credit card)**
belasten; ~ **(cost)** verlangen
cheap billig; ~**er** billiger
check v **(luggage)**
aufgeben; ~ **(on something)**
prüfen; n **(payment)** der
Scheck; ~**-in** das Check-in;
~**ing account** das Girokonto;
~**-out** das Check-out
Cheers! Prost!

chemical toilet die Campingtoilette

chemist [BE] die Apotheke

chest (body part) die Brust; **~ pain** die Brustschmerzen

chewing gum der Kaugummi

child das Kind; **~'s seat** der Kinderstuhl

children's menu das Kindermenü

children's portion die Kinderportion

Chinese *adj* chinesisch

chopsticks die Stäbchen

church die Kirche

cigar die Zigarre

cigarette die Zigarette

class *n* die Klasse; **business ~** die Business-Class; **economy ~** die Economy-Class; **first ~** die erste Klasse

classical music die klassische Musik

clean *v* reinigen; **~** *adj* **(clothes)** sauber; **~ing product** das Reinigungsmittel

clear *v* **(on an ATM)** löschen

cliff die Klippe

cling film [BE] die Klarsichtfolie

close *v* **(a shop)** schließen

closed geschlossen

clothing die Bekleidung; **~ store** das Bekleidungsgeschäft

club *n* der Club

coat der Mantel

coin die Münze

colander das Sieb

cold *n* **(sickness)** die Erkältung; **~** *adj* **(temperature)** kalt

colleague der Kollege

cologne das Kölnischwasser

color *n* die Farbe

comb *n* der Kamm

come *v* kommen

complaint die Beschwerde

computer der Computer

concert das Konzert; **~ hall** die Konzerthalle

condition (medical) die Beschwerden

conditioner (hair) die Spülung

condom das Kondom

conference die Konferenz

confirm bestätigen

congestion (medical) der Blutstau

connect (internet) verbinden

connection (travel/internet) die Verbindung; **~ flight** der Anschlussflug

constipated verstopft

consulate das Konsulat

consultant der Berater

contact *v* kontaktieren

contact lens die Kontaktlinse; **~ solution** Kontaktlinsenlösung

contagious ansteckend
convention hall der Kongresssaal
conveyor belt das Förderband
cook v kochen
cool adj (temperature) kalt
copper n das Kupfer
corkscrew n der Korkenzieher
cost v kosten
cotton die Baumwolle
cough v husten; ~ n der Husten
country code die Landesvorwahl
cover charge der Preis pro Gedeck
cream (ointment) die Creme
credit card die Kreditkarte
crew neck der runde Halsausschnitt
crib das Kinderbett
crystal n (glass) das Kristall
cup n die Tasse
currency die Währung; ~ exchange der Währungsumtausch; ~ exchange office die Wechselstube
current account [BE] das Girokonto
customs der Zoll
cut v schneiden; ~ n (injury) der Schnitt
cute süß
cycling das Radfahren

damage v beschädigen
dance v tanzen; ~ club der Tanzclub; ~ing das Tanzen
dangerous gefährlich
dark adj dunkel
date n (calendar) das Datum
day der Tag
deaf adj taub
debit card die EC-Karte
deck chair der Liegestuhl
declare v (customs) deklarieren
decline v (credit card) ablehnen
deep adj tief
degree (temperature) das Grad
delay v verzögern
delete v (computer) löschen
delicatessen das Feinkostgeschäft
delicious lecker
denim das Denim
dentist der Zahnarzt
denture die Zahnprothese
deodorant das Deodorant
department store das Kaufhaus
departure (plane) der Abflug
deposit v (money) einzahlen; ~ n (bank) die Einzahlung
desert n die Wüste
detergent das Waschmittel
develop v (film) entwickeln

diabetic *adj* diabetisch; *n* der Diabetiker

dial *v* wählen

diamond der Diamant

diaper die Windel

diarrhea der Durchfall

diesel der Diesel

difficult schwierig

digital digital; **~ camera** die Digitalkamera; **~ photo** das Digitalfoto; **~ print** der digitale Ausdruck

dining room das Esszimmer

dinner das Abendessen

direction die Richtung

dirty schmutzig

disabled *adj* **(person)** behindert; **~ accessible [BE]** behindertengerecht

disconnect (computer) trennen

discount *n* der Rabatt; die Ermäßigung

dishes (kitchen) das Geschirr

dishwasher der Geschirrspüler

dishwashing liquid das Geschirrspülmittel

display *n* **(device)** das Display; **~ case** die Vitrine

disposable *n* der Einwegartikel; **~ razor** der Einweg-Rasierer

dive *v* tauchen

diving equipment die Tauchausrüstung

divorce *v* sich scheiden lassen

dizzy *adj* schwindelig

doctor *n* der Arzt

doll *n* die Puppe

dollar (U.S.) der Dollar

domestic inländisch; **~ flight** der Inlandsflug

door die Tür

dormitory der Schlafsaal

double bed das Doppelbett

downtown *n* das Stadtzentrum

dozen das Dutzend

drag lift der Schlepplift

dress (clothing) das Kleid; **~ code** die Kleiderordnung

drink *v* trinken; **~ *n*** das Getränk; **~ menu** die Getränkekarte; **~ing water** das Trinkwasser

drive *v* fahren

driver's license number die Führerscheinnummer

drop *n* **(medicine)** der Tropfen

drowsiness die Schläfrigkeit

dry clean chemisch reinigen; **~er's** die chemische Reinigung

dubbed synchronisiert

during während

duty (tax) der Zoll; **~-free** zollfrei

DVD die DVD

E

ear das Ohr; **~ache** die Ohrenschmerzen
earlier früher
early früh
earring der Ohrring
east n der Osten
easy leicht
eat v essen
economy class die Economy-Class
elbow n der Ellenbogen
electric outlet die Steckdose
elevator der Fahrstuhl
e-mail v eine E-Mail senden; **~** n die E-Mail; **~ address** die E-Mail-Adresse
emergency der Notfall; **~ exit** der Notausgang
empty v entleeren
end v beenden; **~** n das Ende
engaged (person) verlobt
English adj englisch; **~** n **(language)** das Englisch
engrave eingravieren
enjoy genießen
enter v **(place)** eintreten
entertainment die Unterhaltung
entrance der Eingang
envelope der Umschlag
epileptic adj epileptisch; **~** n der Epileptiker
equipment die Ausrüstung
escalator die Rolltreppe
e-ticket das E-Ticket

EU resident der EU-Bürger
euro der Euro
evening n der Abend
excess baggage das Übergepäck
exchange v umtauschen; **~** n **(place)** die Wechselstube; **~ rate** der Wechselkurs
excursion der Ausflug
excuse v entschuldigen
exhausted erschöpft
exit v verlassen; **~** n der Ausgang
expensive teuer
experienced erfahren
expert der Experte
exposure (film) die Belichtung
express adj Express-; **~ bus** der Expressbus; **~ train** der Expresszug
extension (phone) die Durchwahl
extra adj zusätzlich; **~ large** extragroß
extract v **(tooth)** ziehen
eye das Auge
eyebrow wax die Augenbrauenkorrektur

F

face n das Gesicht
facial n die kosmetische Gesichtsbehandlung
family n die Familie
fan n **(appliance)** der Ventilator

far (distance) weit
farm der Bauernhof
far-sighted weitsichtig
fast *adj* schnell
fat free fettfrei
father der Vater
fax *v* faxen; **~** *n* das Fax;
~ number die Faxnummer
fee *n* die Gebühr
feed *v* füttern
ferry *n* die Fähre
fever *n* das Fieber
field (sports) der Platz
fill *v* **(car)** tanken
fill out *v* **(form)** ausfüllen
filling *n* **(tooth)** die Füllung
film *n* **(camera)** der Film
fine *n* **(fee for breaking law)**
die Strafe
finger *n* der Finger; **~nail** der
Fingernagel
fire *n* das Feuer;
~ department die Feuerwehr;
~ door die Feuertür
first *adj* erste; **~ class** erste
Klasse
fit *n* **(clothing)** die Passform
fitting room die
Umkleidekabine
fix *v* **(repair)** reparieren
fixed-price menu das
Festpreismenü
flash photography das
Fotografieren mit Blitzlicht
flashlight das Blitzlicht
flight *n* der Flug

flip-flops die Badelatschen
floor *n* **(level)** die Etage
florist der Florist
flower *n* die Blume
folk music die Volksmusik
food das Essen; **~ processor**
die Küchenmaschine
foot *n* der Fuß
football game [BE] das
Fußballspiel
for für
forecast *n* die Vorhersage
forest *n* der Wald
fork *n* die Gabel
form *n* **(document)** das
Formular
formula (baby) die
Babynahrung
fort die Festung
fountain *n* der Springbrunnen
free *adj* frei
freelance work
die freiberufliche Arbeit
freezer der Gefrierschrank
fresh frisch
friend der Freund
frozen food die Tiefkühlkost
frying pan die Bratpfanne
full-time *adj* Vollzeit-

G

game *n* das Spiel
garage *n* **(parking)** die
Garage; **~** *n* **(for repairs)** die
Autowerkstatt

garbage bag der Abfallbeutel
gas (car) das Benzin;
~ **station** die Tankstelle
gate (airport) das Gate
gay *adj* **(homosexual)** schwul;
~ **bar** die Schwulenbar;
~ **club** der Schwulenclub
gel *n* **(hair)** das Gel
generic drug das Generikum
German *adj* deutsch; ~ *n*
(language) das Deutsch
Germany Deutschland
get off (a train/bus/subway)
aussteigen
gift *n* das Geschenk; ~ **shop**
der Geschenkwarenladen
girl das Mädchen; ~**friend**
die Freundin
give *v* geben
glass (drinking) das Glas;
~ **(material)** das Glas
glasses die Brille
go *v* **(somewhere)** gehen
gold *n* das Gold
golf *n* das Golf; ~ **course**
der Golfplatz; ~ **tournament**
das Golfturnier
good *adj* gut; ~ *n* die Ware;
~ **afternoon** guten Tag
~ **day** guten Tag; ~ **evening**
guten Abend; ~ **morning**
guten Morgen; ~**bye** auf
Wiedersehen
gram das Gramm
grandchild das Enkelkind
grandparents die Großeltern

gray *adj* grau
green *adj* grün
grocery store das
Lebensmittelgeschäft
ground floor das Erdgeschoss
groundcloth die Unterlegplane
group *n* die Gruppe
guide *n* **(book)** der
Reiseführer; ~ *n* **(person)**
der Fremdenführer ~ **dog** der
Blindenhund
gym *n* **(place)** der Fitnessraum
gynecologist der Gynäkologe

H

hair das Haar; ~**brush**
die Haarbürste; ~**cut** der
Haarschnitt; ~ **dryer** der Fön;
~ **salon** der Friseursalon;
~**spray** das Haarspray; ~**style**
die Frisur; ~ **stylist** der Friseur
halal halal
half *adj* halb; ~ *n* die Hälfte;
~ **hour** die halbe Stunde;
~**-kilo** das halbe Kilo
hammer *n* der Hammer
hand *n* die Hand; ~ **luggage**
das Handgepäck; ~ **wash** die
Handwäsche; ~**bag [BE]** die
Handtasche
handicapped behindert;
~**-accessible**
behindertengerecht
hangover der Kater
happy glücklich

hat der Hut
have *v* haben; **~ sex** Sex haben
hay fever der Heuschnupfen
head (body part) *n* der Kopf;
~ache die Kopfschmerzen;
~phones die Kopfhörer
health die Gesundheit; **~ food
store** das Reformhaus
hearing impaired
hörgeschädigt
heart das Herz; **~ condition**
die Herzkrankheit
heat *v* heizen; **~er** das
Heizgerät; **~ing [BE]** die
Heizung
hectare der Hektar
hello Hallo
helmet der Helm
help *v* helfen; **~** *n* die Hilfe
here hier
hi Hallo
high hoch; **~chair** der
Kindersitz; **~lights (hair)**
die Strähnchen; **~way**
die Autobahn
hiking boots die
Wanderschuhe
hill *n* der Berg
hire *v* **[BE] (a car)** mieten;
~ car [BE] das Mietauto
hockey das Hockey
holiday [BE] der Urlaub
horsetrack die
Pferderennbahn
hospital das Krankenhaus
hostel die Jugendherberge

hot (spicy) scharf;
~ (temperature) heiß;
~ spring heiße Quelle;
~ water heißes Wasser
hotel das Hotel
hour die Stunde
house *n* das Haus; **~hold
goods** die Haushaltswaren;
~keeping services der
Hotelservice
how wie; **~ much** wie viel
hug *v* umarmen
hungry hungrig
hurt *v* wehtun
husband der Ehemann

I

ibuprofen das Ibuprofen
ice *n* das Eis; **~ hockey** das
Eishockey
icy eisig
identification die Identifikation
ill krank
in in
include *v* beinhalten
indoor pool (public) das
Hallenbad
inexpensive preisgünstig
infected infiziert
information (phone) die
Auskunft; **~ desk** die
Information
insect das Insekt; **~ bite** der
Insektenstich; **~ repellent** der
Insektenschutz

insert v **(card)** einführen
insomnia die Schlaflosigkeit
instant message die instant Message
insulin das Insulin
insurance die Versicherung; **~ card** die Versicherungskarte; **~ company** die Versicherungsgesellschaft
interesting interessant
intermediate fortgeschritten
international international; **~ flight** der internationale Flug; **~ student card** der internationale Studentenausweis
internet das Internet; **~ cafe** das Internetcafé; **~ service** der Internetservice
interpreter der Dolmetscher
intersection die Kreuzung
intestine der Darm
introduce v **(person)** vorstellen
invoice n **[BE]** die Rechnung
Ireland das Irland
Irish adj irisch
iron v bügeln; **~** n **(clothes)** das Bügeleisen
Italian adj italienisch

J

jacket n die Jacke
Japanese adj japanisch
jar n **(for jam etc.)** das Glas
jaw n der Kiefer

jazz n der Jazz; **~ club** der Jazzclub
jeans die Jeans
jet ski n die Jet-Ski
jeweler der Juwelier
jewelry der Schmuck
join v **(go with somebody)** mitkommen
joint n **(body part)** das Gelenk

K

key n der Schlüssel; **~ card** die Schlüsselkarte; **~ring** der Schlüsselring
kiddie pool das Kinderbecken
kidney (body part) die Niere
kilo das Kilo; **~gram** das Kilogramm; **~meter** der Kilometer
kiss v küssen
kitchen die Küche; **~ foil [BE]** die Aluminiumfolie
knee n das Knie
knife das Messer
kosher adj koscher

L

lace n **(fabric)** die Spitze
lactose intolerant laktoseintolerant
lake der See
large groß
last adj letzte
late (time) spät

launderette [BE] der Waschsalon
laundromat der Waschsalon
laundry (place) die Wäscherei
~ service der Wäscheservice
lawyer *n* der Anwalt
leather *n* das Leder
leave *v* **(hotel)** abreisen; **~ (plane)** abfliegen
left *adj, adv* **(direction)** links
leg *n* das Bein
lens die Linse
less weniger
lesson *n* die Lektion; **take ~s** Unterricht nehmen
letter *n* der Brief
library die Bücherei
life jacket die Schwimmweste
lifeguard der Rettungsschwimmer
lift *n* **[BE]** der Fahrstuhl; **~** *n* **(ride)** die Mitfahrgelegenheit; **~ pass** der Liftpass
light *n* **(cigarette)** das Feuer; **~** *n* **(overhead)** die Lampe; **~bulb** die Glühbirne
lighter *n* das Feuerzeug
like *v* mögen
line *n* **(train/bus)** die Linie
linen das Leinen
lip *n* die Lippe
liquor store das Spirituosengeschäft
liter der Liter
little wenig
live *v* leben; **~ music** Livemusik

liver (body part) die Leber
loafers die Halbschuhe
local *n* **(person)** der Einheimische
lock *v* abschließen; **~** *n* das Schloss
locker das Schließfach
log off *v* **(computer)** abmelden
log on *v* **(computer)** anmelden
long *adj* lang; **~-sighted [BE]** weitsichtig; **~-sleeved** langärmlig
look *v* schauen; **~ for something** etwas suchen
loose (fit) locker
lose *v* **(something)** verlieren
lost verloren; **~-and-found** das Fundbüro
lotion die Lotion
louder lauter
love *v* **(someone)** lieben; **~** *n* die Liebe
low *adj* niedrig
luggage das Gepäck; **~ cart** der Gepäckwagen; **~ locker** das Gepäckschließfach; **~ ticket** der Gepäckschein
lunch *n* das Mittagessen
lung die Lunge
luxury car das Luxusauto

M

machine washable maschinenwaschbar
magazine das Magazin

magnificent großartig

mail _v_ mit der Post schicken; ~ _n_ die Post; **~box** der Briefkasten

main attraction die Hauptattraktion

main course das Hauptgericht

mall das Einkaufszentrum

man (adult male) der Mann

manager der Manager

manicure _n_ die Maniküre

manual car das Auto mit Gangschaltung

map _n_ die Karte; ~ _n_ **(town)** der Stadtplan

market _n_ der Markt

married verheiratet

marry heiraten

mass _n_ **(church service)** die Messe

massage _n_ die Massage

match _n_ das Spiel

meal die Mahlzeit

measure _v_ **(someone)** Maß nehmen

measuring cup der Messbecher

measuring spoon der Messlöffel

mechanic _n_ der Mechaniker

medication (drugs) die Medikamente

medicine das Medikament

medium (steak) medium

meet _v_ treffen

meeting _n_ **(business)** das Meeting; **~ room** das Konferenzzimmer

membership card der Mitgliedsausweis

memorial (place) das Denkmal

memory card die Speicherkarte

mend _v_ **(clothes)** ausbessern

menstrual cramps die Menstruationskrämpfe

menu (restaurant) die Speisekarte

message die Nachricht

meter _n_ **(parking)** die Parkuhr; ~ _n_ **(measure)** der Meter

microwave _n_ die Mikrowelle

midday [BE] der Mittag

midnight die Mitternacht

mileage die Meilenzahl

mini-bar die Mini-Bar

minute die Minute

missing (not there) weg

mistake _n_ der Fehler

mobile home der Wohnwagen

mobile phone [BE] das Handy

mobility die Mobilität

monastery das Kloster

money das Geld

month der Monat

mop _n_ der Wischmopp

moped das Moped

more mehr

morning _n_ der Morgen

mosque die Moschee

mother _n_ die Mutter

motion sickness die
Reisekrankheit
motor *n* der Motor;
~ **boat** das Motorboot;
~**cycle** das Motorrad;
~**way [BE]** die Autobahn
mountain der Berg;
~ **bike** das Mountainbike
mousse (hair) der
Schaumfestiger
mouth *n* der Mund
movie der Film; ~ **theater**
das Kino
mug *v* überfallen
multiple-trip ticket
der Mehrfachfahrschein
muscle *n* der Muskel
museum das Museum
music die Musik; ~ **store**
das Musikgeschäft

N

nail file die Nagelfeile
nail salon das Nagelstudio
name *n* der Name
napkin die Serviette
nappy [BE] die Windel
nationality die Nationalität
nature preserve das
Naturreservat
nausea die Übelkeit
nauseous übel
near nahe; ~-**sighted**
kurzsichtig
nearby in der Nähe von

neck *n* der Nacken
necklace die Kette
need *v* brauchen
newspaper die Zeitung
newsstand der Zeitungskiosk
next *adj* nächste
nice schön
night die Nacht; ~**club** der
Nachtclub
no nein; ~ **(not any)** kein
non-alcoholic nichtalkoholisch
non-smoking *adj* Nichtraucher
noon *n* der Mittag
north *n* der Norden
nose die Nase
note *n* **[BE] (money)** der
Geldschein
nothing nichts
notify *v* benachrichtigen
novice der Anfänger
now jetzt
number *n* die Nummer
nurse *n* die
Krankenschwester

O

office das Büro; ~ **hours**
die Bürozeiten
off-licence [BE] das
Spirituosengenschäft
oil *n* das Öl
OK okay
old *adj* alt
on the corner an der Ecke
once (one time) einmal

one ein; **(counting)** eins;
  ~-day (ticket) Tages-;
  ~-way ticket (airline)
  das einfache Ticket,
  (bus/train/subway) die
  Einzelfahrkarte; **~-way street**
  die Einbahnstraße
only nur
open v öffnen; **~** adj offen
opera die Oper;
  ~ house das Opernhaus
opposite n das Gegenteil
optician der Optiker
orange adj **(color)** orange
orchestra das Orchester
order v **(restaurant)** bestellen
outdoor pool das Freibad
outside prep draußen
over prep **(direction)** über;
  ~done (meat) zu lang
  gebraten; **~heat** v **(car)**
  überhitzen; **~look** n
  (scenic place) der
  Aussichtsplatz; **~night**
  über Nacht; **~-the-counter**
  (medication) rezeptfrei
oxygen treatment die
  Sauerstoffbehandlung

P

p.m. nachmittags
pacifier der Schnuller
pack v packen
package n das Paket
pad n **[BE]** die Monatsbinde

paddling pool [BE] das
  Kinderbecken
pain der Schmerz
pajamas der Pyjama
palace der Palast
pants die Hose
pantyhose die Strumpfhose
paper n **(material)** das Papier;
  ~ towel das Papierhandtuch
paracetamol [BE] das
  Paracetamol
park v parken; **~** n der Park;
  ~ing garage das Parkhaus;
  ~ing lot der Parkplatz;
  ~ing meter die Parkuhr
parliament building das
  Parlamentsgebäude
part (for car) das Teil;
  ~-time adj Teilzeit-
pass through v **(travel)**
  durchreisen
passenger der Passagier
passport der Reisepass;
  ~ control die Passkontrolle
password das Passwort
pastry shop die Konditorei
patch v **(clothing)** ausbessern
path der Pfad
pay v bezahlen; **~phone**
  das öffentliche Telefon
peak n **(of a mountain)**
  der Gipfel
pearl n die Perle
pedestrian n der Fußgänger
pediatrician der Kinderarzt
pedicure n die Pediküre

pen n der Stift
penicillin das Penicillin
penis der Penis
per pro; **~ day** pro Tag;
  ~ hour pro Stunde;
  ~ night pro Nacht;
  ~ week pro Woche
perfume n das Parfüm
period (menstrual) die
  Periode; **~ (of time)** der
  Zeitraum
permit v erlauben
petrol [BE] das Benzin;
  ~ station [BE] die Tankstelle
pewter das Zinn
pharmacy die Apotheke
phone v anrufen; **~** n das
  Telefon; **~ call** das Telefonat;
  ~ card die Telefonkarte;
  ~ number die Telefonnummer
photo das Foto;
  ~copy die Fotokopie;
  ~graphy die Fotografie
pick up v **(person)** abholen
picnic area der Rastplatz
piece n das Stück
Pill (birth control) die Pille
pillow n das Kissen
pink adj rosa
piste [BE] die Piste; **~ map**
  [BE] der Pistenplan
pizzeria die Pizzeria
place v **(a bet)** abgeben
plane n das Flugzeug
plastic wrap die
  Klarsichtfolie

plate n der Teller
platform [BE] (train) der
  Bahnsteig
platinum n das Platin
play v spielen; **~** n **(theatre)**
  das Stück; **~ground** der
  Spielplatz; **~pen** der Laufstall
please adv bitte
pleasure n die Freude
plunger die Saugglocke
plus size die Übergröße
pocket n die Tasche
poison n das Gift
poles (skiing) die Stöcke
police die Polizei;
  ~ report der Polizeibericht;
  ~ station das Polizeirevier
pond n der Teich
pool n der Pool
pop music die Popmusik
portion n die Portion
post n **[BE]** die Post;
  ~ office die Post;
  ~box [BE] der Briefkasten;
  ~card die Postkarte
pot n der Topf
pottery die Töpferwaren
pound n **(weight)** das Pfund;
  ~ (British sterling) das
  Pfund
pregnant schwanger
prescribe (medication)
  verschreiben
prescription das Rezept
press v **(clothing)** bügeln
price n der Preis

print v drucken; ~ n der Ausdruck

problem das Problem

produce n das Erzeugnis; ~ **store** das Lebensmittelgeschäft

prohibit verbieten

pronounce aussprechen

Protestant der Protestant

public adj öffentlich

pull v ziehen

purple adj violett

purse n die Handtasche

push v drücken; ~**chair [BE]** der Kinderwagen

Q

quality n die Qualität

question n die Frage

quiet adj leise

R

racetrack die Rennbahn

racket n **(sports)** der Schläger

railway station [BE] der Bahnhof

rain n der Regen; ~**coat** die Regenjacke; ~**forest** der Regenwald; ~**y** regnerisch

rap n **(music)** der Rap

rape v vergewaltigen; ~ n die Vergewaltigung

rare selten

rash n der Ausschlag

ravine die Schlucht

razor blade die Rasierklinge

reach v erreichen

ready bereit

real adj echt

receipt n die Quittung

receive v erhalten

reception (hotel) die Rezeption

recharge v aufladen

recommend empfehlen

recommendation die Empfehlung

recycling das Recycling

red adj rot

refrigerator der Kühlschrank

region die Region

registered mail das Einschreiben

regular n **(fuel)** das Normalbenzin

relationship die Beziehung

rent v mieten; ~ n die Miete

rental car das Mietauto

repair v reparieren

repeat v wiederholen

reservation die Reservierung; ~ **desk** der Reservierungsschalter

reserve v **(hotel)** reservieren

restaurant das Restaurant

restroom die Toilette

retired adj **(from work)** in Rente

return v **(something)** zurückgeben; ~ n **[BE] (trip)** die Hin- und Rückfahrt

reverse *v* **(the charges) [BE]** ein R-Gespräch führen
rib *n* **(body part)** die Rippe
right *adj, adv* **(direction)** rechts; **~ of way** die Vorfahrt
ring *n* der Ring
river der Fluss
road map die Straßenkarte
rob *v* berauben
robbed beraubt
romantic *adj* romantisch
room *n* das Zimmer; **~ key** der Zimmerschlüssel; **~ service** der Zimmerservice
round trip die Hin- und Rückfahrt
route *n* die Route
rowboat das Ruderboot
rubbing alcohol der Franzbranntwein
rubbish *n* **[BE]** der Abfall; **~ bag [BE]** der Abfallbeutel
rugby das Rugby
ruin *n* die Ruine
rush *n* die Eile

S

sad traurig
safe *adj* **(protected)** sicher; **~ n (thing)** der Safe
sales tax die Mehrwertsteuer
same *adj* gleiche
sandals die Sandalen
sanitary napkin die Monatsbinde

sauna die Sauna
sauté *v* sautieren
save *v* **(computer)** speichern
savings (account) das Sparkonto
scanner der Scanner
scarf der Schal
schedule *v* planen; **~ n** der Plan
school *n* die Schule
science die Wissenschaft
scissors die Schere
sea das Meer
seat *n* der Sitzplatz
security die Sicherheit
see *v* sehen
self-service *n* die Selbstbedienung
sell *v* verkaufen
seminar das Seminar
send *v* senden
senior citizen der Rentner
separated (person) getrennt lebend
serious ernst
service (in a restaurant) die Bedienung
sexually transmitted disease (STD) die sexuell übertragbare Krankheit
shampoo *n* das Shampoo
sharp *adj* scharf
shaving cream die Rasiercreme
sheet *n* **(bed)** die Bettwäsche
ship *v* versenden
shirt das Hemd

shoe store das Schuhgeschäft
shoe der Schuh
shop *v* einkaufen;
~ *n* das Geschäft
shopping *n* das Einkaufen;
~ **area** das Einkaufszentrum;
~ **centre [BE]** das
Einkaufszentrum;
~ **mall** das Einkaufszentrum
short kurz; ~-**sleeved**
kurzärmelig
shorts die kurze Hose
short-sighted [BE]
kurzsichtig
shoulder *n* die Schulter
show *v* zeigen
shower *n* (**bath**) die Dusche
shrine der Schrein
sick *adj* krank
side *n* die Seite; ~ **dish**
die Beilage; ~ **effect** die
Nebenwirkung; ~ **order** die
Beilage
sightseeing das Besichtigen
von Sehenswürdigkeiten;
~ **tour** die Besichtigungstour
sign *v* (**document**)
unterschreiben
silk die Seide
silver *n* das Silber
single *adj* (**person**)
alleinstehend;
~ **bed** das Einzelbett;
~ **print** der Einzelabzug;
~ **room** das Einzelzimmer
sink *n* das Waschbecken

sister die Schwester
sit *v* sitzen
size *n* die Größe
ski *v* Ski fahren; ~ *n* der Ski;
~ **lift** der Skilift
skin *n* die Haut
skirt *n* der Rock
sleep *v* schlafen; ~**er car**
der Schlafwagen; ~**ing bag**
der Schlafsack; ~**ing car [BE]**
der Schlafwagen
slice *n* die Scheibe
slippers die Pantoffeln
slower langsamer
slowly langsam
small klein
smoke *v* rauchen
smoking (area) Raucher-
snack bar der Imbiss
sneakers die Turnschuhe
snorkeling equipment die
Schnorchelausrüstung
snowboard *n* das
Snowboard
snowshoe *n* der
Schneeschuh
snowy verschneit
soap *n* die Seife
soccer der Fußball
sock die Socke
**some (with singular
nouns)** etwas; ~ **(with
plural nouns)** einige
soother [BE] der Schnuller
sore throat die
Halsschmerzen

south *n* der Süden
souvenir *n* das Souvenir;
~ **store** das Souvenirgeschäft
spa das Wellness-Center
spatula der Spatel
speak *v* sprechen
specialist (doctor) der
Spezialist
specimen die Probe
speeding die
Geschwindigkeitsüberschreitung
spell *v* buchstabieren
spicy scharf; ~ **(not bland)**
würzig
spine (body part) die
Wirbelsäule
spoon *n* der Löffel
sporting goods store das
Sportgeschäft
sports der Sport; ~ **massage**
die Sportmassage
sprain *n* die Verstauchung
stadium das Stadion
stairs die Treppe
stamp *v* **(ticket)** entwerten;
~ *n* **(postage)** die Briefmarke
start *v* beginnen
starter [BE] die Vorspeise
station *n* **(stop)** die Haltestelle;
bus ~ der Busbahnhof;
gas ~ die Tankstelle;
petrol ~ **[BE]** die Tankstelle;
subway ~ die U-Bahn-
Haltestelle; **train** ~ der
Bahnhof
statue die Statue

steakhouse das Steakhouse
steal *v* stehlen
steep *adj* steil
sterling silver das
Sterlingsilber
sting *n* der Stich
stolen gestohlen
stomach der Magen;
~**ache** die Bauchschmerzen
stool (bowel movement) der
Stuhlgang
stop *v* **(bus)** anhalten;
~ *n* **(transportation)** die
Haltestelle
store directory (mall) der
Übersichtsplan
storey [BE] die Etage
stove *n* der Herd
straight *adv* **(direction)**
geradeaus
strange seltsam
stream *n* der Strom
stroller (baby) der
Kinderwagen
student (university) der
Student; ~ **(school)** der
Schüler
study *v* studieren;
~**ing** *n* das Studieren
stuffed gefüllt
stunning umwerfend
subtitle *n* der Untertitel
subway die U-Bahn; ~ **station**
die U-Bahn Haltestelle
suit *n* der Anzug; ~**case** der
Koffer

sun *n* die Sonne; **~block** das Sonnenschutzmittel; **~burn** der Sonnenbrand; **~glasses** die Sonnenbrille; **~ny** sonnig; **~screen** die Sonnencreme; **~stroke** der Sonnenstich
super *n* (fuel) das Superbenzin; **~market** der Supermarkt
surfboard das Surfboard
surgical spirit [BE] der Franzbranntwein
swallow *v* schlucken
sweater der Pullover
sweatshirt das Sweatshirt
sweet *n* [BE] die Süßigkeit; **~** *adj* (taste) süß
swelling die Schwellung
swim *v* schwimmen; **~suit** der Badeanzug
symbol (keyboard) das Zeichen
synagogue die Synagoge

T

table *n* der Tisch
tablet (medicine) die Tablette
take *v* nehmen
tampon *n* der Tampon
taste *v* (test) kosten
taxi *n* das Taxi
team *n* das Team
teaspoon der Teelöffel
telephone *n* das Telefon
temple (religious) der Tempel

temporary vorübergehend
tennis das Tennis
tent *n* das Zelt; **~ peg** der Zelthering; **~ pole** die Zeltstange
terminal *n* (airport) der Terminal
terrible schrecklich
text *v* (send a message) eine SMS schicken; **~** *n* der Text
thank *v* danken; **~ you** vielen Dank
the der ♂, das (neuter), die ♀
theater das Theater
theft der Diebstahl
there dort
thief der Dieb
thigh der Oberschenkel
thirsty durstig
this dieser ♂, dieses (neuter), diese ♀
throat der Hals
thunderstorm das Gewitter
ticket *n* die Fahrkarte; **~ office** der Fahrkartenschalter
tie *n* (clothing) die Krawatte
tight (fit) eng
tights [BE] die Strumpfhose
time die Zeit; **~table** [BE] (transportation) der Fahrplan
tire *n* der Reifen
tired müde
tissue das Gewebe
tobacconist der Tabakhändler

today *adv* heute
toe *n* der Zeh
toenail der Zehnagel
toilet [BE] die Toilette;
~ **paper** das Toilettenpapier
tomorrow *adv* morgen
tongue *n* die Zunge
tonight heute Abend
to (direction) zu
tooth der Zahn
toothpaste die Zahnpasta
total *n* (amount) der
Gesamtbetrag
tough *adj* (food) zäh
tour *n* die Tour
tourist der Tourist;
~ **information office** das
Touristeninformationsbüro
tow truck der
Abschleppwagen
towel *n* das Handtuch
tower *n* der Turm
town die Stadt; ~ **hall**
das Rathaus; ~ **map** der
Stadtplan; ~ **square** der
Rathausplatz
toy das Spielzeug;
~ **store** der Spielzeugladen
track *n* (train) der Bahnsteig
traditional traditionell
traffic light die Ampel
trail *n* (ski) die Piste;
~ **map** der Pistenplan
trailer (car) der Anhänger
train *n* der Zug;
~ **station** der Bahnhof

transfer *v* (change trains/
flights) umsteigen;
~ (money) überweisen
translate übersetzen
trash *n* der Abfall
travel *n* das Reisen;
~ **agency** das Reisebüro;
~ **sickness** die Reisekrankheit;
~**ers check** [cheque BE] der
Reisescheck
tree der Baum
trim (hair) *v* nachschneiden
trip *n* die Reise
trolley [BE] (grocery store)
der Einkaufswagen; ~ [BE]
(luggage) der Gepäckwagen
trousers [BE] die Hose
T-shirt das T-Shirt
tumble dry
maschinentrocknen
turn off *v* (device)
ausschalten
turn on *v* (device) anschalten
TV der Fernseher
tyre [BE] der Reifen

U

ugly hässlich
umbrella der Regenschirm
unattended unbeaufsichtigt
unbranded medication [BE]
das Generikum
unconscious
(faint) bewusstlos
underdone halb gar

underground *n* [BE] die U-Bahn; **~ station** [BE] die U-Bahn-Haltestelle
underpants [BE] der Slip
understand *v* verstehen
underwear die Unterwäsche
unemployed arbeitslos
United Kingdom (U.K.) das Großbritannien
United States (U.S.) die Vereinigten Staaten
university die Universität
unleaded (gas) bleifrei
upset stomach die Magenverstimmung
urgent dringend
urine der Urin
use *v* benutzen
username der Benutzername
utensil das Haushaltsgerät

V

vacancy (room) das freie Zimmer
vacation der Urlaub
vaccination die Impfung
vacuum cleaner der Staubsauger
vagina die Vagina
vaginal infection die vaginale Entzündung
valid gültig
valley das Tal
valuable *adj* wertvoll
value *n* der Wert

van der Kleintransporter
VAT [BE] die Mehrwertsteuer
vegan *n* der Veganer; **~** *adj* vegan
vegetarian *n* der Vegetarier; **~** *adj* vegetarisch
vehicle registration die Fahrzeugregistrierung
viewpoint (scenic) [BE] der Aussichtsplatz
village das Dorf
vineyard das Weingut
visa das Visum
visit *v* besuchen; **~ing hours** die Besuchszeiten
visually impaired sehbehindert
vitamin das Vitamin
V-neck der V-Ausschnitt
volleyball game das Volleyballspiel
vomit *v* erbrechen; **~ing** das Erbrechen

W

wait *v* warten; **~** *n* die Wartezeit
waiter der Kellner
waiting room der Warteraum
waitress die Kellnerin
wake *v* wecken; **~-up call** der Weckruf
walk *v* spazieren gehen; **~** *n* der Spaziergang; **~ing route** die Wanderroute
wall clock die Wanduhr
wallet die Geldbörse

war memorial
das Kriegsdenkmal
warm *v* **(something)** erwärmen;
~ *adj* **(temperature)** warm
washing machine die
Waschmaschine
watch *v* beobachten
water ski *n* der Wasserski
waterfall der Wasserfall
wax *v* **(hair)** mit Wachs
entfernen (Haare)
weather *n* das Wetter
week die Woche; ~**end** das
Wochenende
weekly wöchentlich
welcome *adj* willkommen;
you're ~ gern geschehen
well-rested ausgeruht
west *n* der Westen
what was
wheelchair der Rollstuhl;
~ **ramp** die Rollstuhlrampe
when *adv* **(at what time)** wann
where wo
white *adj* weiß; ~ **gold** das
Weißgold
who (question) wer
widowed verwitwet
wife die Ehefrau
window das Fenster;
~ **case** das Schaufenster

windsurfer (board) das
Surfbrett
wine list die Weinkarte
wireless wireless; ~ **phone**
das schnurlose Telefon
with mit
withdraw *v* **(money)** abheben;
~**al (bank)** die Abhebung
without ohne
woman die Frau
wool die Wolle
work *v* arbeiten
wrap *v* einpacken
wrist das Handgelenk
write *v* schreiben

Y

year das Jahr
yellow *adj* gelb; ~ **gold** *n* das
Gelbgold
yes ja
yesterday *adv* gestern
young *adj* jung
youth hostel die
Jugendherberge

Z

zoo der Zoo

German–English Dictionary

A

der **Abend** evening
das **Abendessen** dinner
der **Abfall** n trash [rubbish BE]
der **Abfallbeutel** garbage
[rubbish BE] bag
abfliegen v leave (plane)
der **Abflug** departure (plane)
abgeben v place (a bet)
abheben v withdraw (money)
die **Abhebung** withdrawal (bank)
abholen v pick up (something)
ablehnen v decline (credit card)
abmelden v log off (computer)
der **Abschleppwagen** tow truck
abschließen v lock (door)
der **Adapter** adapter
die **Adresse** n address
das **Aftershave** aftershave
die **Agentur** agency
AIDS AIDS
die **Akupunktur** n acupuncture
akzeptieren v accept
allein alone; **~stehend** single
(person)
allergisch allergic;
die **allergische Reaktion**
allergic reaction
alt adj old
das **Alter** n age
die **Alternativroute** alternate
route

die **Aluminiumfolie** aluminum
[kitchen BE] foil
amerikanisch American
die **Ampel** traffic light
anämisch anemic
die **Anästhesie** anesthesia
der **Anfänger** beginner/novice
angreifen v attack
anhalten v stop
der **Anhänger** trailer
ankommen arrive
die **Ankunft** arrival
anmelden v log on (computer)
der **Anruf** n call
anrufen v call
anschalten v turn on (device)
ansteckend contagious
das **Antibiotikum** n antibiotic
das **Antiquitätengeschäft**
antiques store
antiseptisch antiseptic
der **Anwalt** lawyer
die **Anzahlung** n deposit
(car rental)
der **Anzug** n suit
das **Apartment** apartment
die **Apotheke** pharmacy
[chemist BE]
arbeiten v work
arbeitslos adj unemployed
der **Arm** n arm (body part)
die **Aromatherapie**
aromatherapy
die **Arterie** artery
die **Arthritis** arthritis
der **Arzt** doctor

asiatisch Asian
das Aspirin aspirin
asthmatisch asthmatic
atmen breathe (place)
attraktiv attractive
auf Wiedersehen goodbye
aufladen *v* recharge
das Auge eye
ausbessern *v* mend (clothing)
der Ausfluss discharge (bodily fluid)
ausfüllen *v* fill out (form)
der Ausgang *n* exit
ausgeschlafen well-rested
die Auskunft information (phone)
die Ausrüstung equipment
ausschalten turn off (device)
der Ausschlag rash
der Aussichtsplatz viewpoint [BE]
aussprechen pronounce
aussteigen get off (a train/ bus/subway)
Australien Australia
der Australier Australian
das Auto car; **~ mit Automatikschaltung** automatic car; **~ mit Gangschaltung** manual car
die Autobahn highway [motorway BE]
automatisch automatic
der Autositz car seat
die Autovermietung car rental [hire BE]

B

das Baby baby
die Babyflasche baby bottle
die Babynahrung formula (baby)
das Baby-Pflegetuch baby wipe
der Babysitter babysitter
backen bake
die Bäckerei bakery
das Bad bathroom
der Badeanzug swimsuit
die Badelatschen flip-flops
der Bahnhof train [railway BE] station
der Bahnsteig track [platform BE]
das Ballett ballet
die Bank bank (money)
der Bankautomat ATM
die Bankkarte ATM card
die Bar bar (place)
das Bargeld *n* cash
der Baseball baseball (game)
der Basketball basketball (game)
die Batterie battery
die Bauchschmerzen stomachache
der Bauernhof *n* farm
der Baum tree
die Baumwolle cotton
die Beaufsichtigung supervision
die Bedienung service (in a restaurant)
beenden *v* exit (computer)

beginnen begin
behindert handicapped;
~**engerecht** handicapped
[disabled BE]-accessible
beige *adj* beige
die Beilage side order
das Bein leg
beinhalten include (tax)
die Bekleidung clothing
das Bekleidungsgeschäft
clothing store
belasten *v* charge (credit card)
belästigen bother
die Belichtung exposure (film)
benachrichtigen notify
benutzen *v* use
der Benutzername username
das Benzin gas [petrol BE]
beobachten *v* watch
der Berater consultant
berauben rob
beraubt robbed
bereit ready
der Berg hill; ~ mountain
beschädigen *v* damage
beschädigt damaged
die Beschwerde complaint
die Beschwerden condition
(medical)
der Besen broom
die Besichtigungstour
sightseeing tour
besser better
bestätigen confirm
beste *adj* best
bestellen *v* order (restaurant)
besuchen *v* visit

die Besuchszeiten visiting hours
das Bett *n* bed
die Bettwäsche sheets
bewusstlos unconscious
(condition)
bezahlen pay
die Beziehung relationship
der BH bra
der Bikini bikini
billig cheap
billiger cheaper
bitte please
die Blase bladder
blau *adj* blue
bleifrei unleaded (gas)
der Blinddarm appendix (body
part)
der Blindenhund guide dog
das Blitzlicht flashlight
die Blume *n* flower
die Bluse blouse
das Blut blood
der Blutdruck blood pressure
bluten bleed
der Blutstau congestion
das Boot boat
die Bordkarte boarding pass
der botanische Garten
botanical garden
der Boxkampf boxing match
die Bratpfanne frying pan
brauchen *v* need
braun *adj* brown
brechen *v* break
die Bremse brakes (car)
brennen *v* burn
der Brief letter

der Briefkasten mailbox
  [postbox BE]
die Briefmarke *n* stamp
  (postage)
die Brille glasses (optical)
bringen bring
britisch British
die Brosche brooch
die Brücke bridge
der Bruder brother
die Brust breast; ~ chest
  ~schmerzen chest pain
das Buch *n* book
die Bücherei library
der Buchladen bookstore
buchstabieren *v* spell
das Bügeleisen *n* iron (clothes)
bügeln *v* iron
das Büro office
die Bürozeiten office hours
der Bus bus; ~**bahnhof** bus
  station; ~**fahrschein** bus ticket
die Bushaltestelle bus stop;
die Business-Class business
  class
die Bustour bus tour

C

das Café cafe (place)
campen *v* camp
der Campingkocher camping
  stove
der Campingplatz campsite
die Campingtoilette chemical
  toilet

der Canyon canyon
das Casino casino
die CD CD
Celsius Celsius
das Check-in check-in
das Check-out check-out
chinesisch Chinese
der Club *n* club
der Computer computer
die Creme *n* cream (ointment)

D

danken thank
der Darm intestine
das (neuter) the
das Datum *n* date (calendar)
die Decke blanket
das Denkmal memorial (place)
der ♂ the
das Deutsch German;
  ~**land** Germany
der Diabetiker *n* diabetic
der Diamant diamond
die ♀ the
der Dieb thief; ~**stahl** theft
diese ♀ this
der Diesel diesel
dieser ♂ this
dieses (neuter) this
digital digital
der Digitaldruck digital print
das Digitalfoto digital photo
die Digitalkamera digital
  camera

das Display n display
Dollar dollar (U.S.)
der Dolmetscher interpreter
das Doppelbett double bed
das Dorf village
dort there
der Dosenöffner can opener
draußen outside
dringend urgent
drucken v print
drücken v push
dunkel adj dark
der Durchfall diarrhea
durchreisen pass through
durstig thirsty
die Dusche n shower
das Dutzend dozen
die DVD DVD

echt real
die EC-Karte debit card
die Ecke n corner; **an der Ecke** on the corner
die Economy-Class economy class
die Ehefrau wife
der Ehemann husband
die Eile n rush
die Einbahnstraße one-way street
einbrechen v break in (burglary)
einchecken v check in
einführen v insert
der Eingang entrance

eingravieren engrave
der Einheimische n local (person)
einkaufen v shop
das Einkaufen shopping
der Einkaufskorb basket (grocery store)
der Einkaufswagen cart [trolley BE] (grocery store)
das Einkaufszentrum shopping mall [centre BE]; ~ shopping area (town)
einlösen v cash (check)
einmal once
einpacken v wrap (parcel)
eins one
das Einschreiben registered mail
einsteigen v board (bus)
eintreten v enter
der Eintritt admission (fee)
der Einwegartikel n disposable
der Einweg-Rasierer disposable razor
einzahlen v deposit (money)
die Einzahlung n deposit (bank)
der Einzelabzug single print
das Einzelbett single bed
das Einzelzimmer single room
das Eis n ice; ~**hockey** ice hockey
der Ellenbogen elbow
die E-Mail n e-mail; ~**-Adresse** e-mail address; ~ **senden** v e-mail
empfehlen recommend
die Empfehlung recommendation

eng tight (fit)
englisch English
der Enkel grandchild
entleeren v empty
entschuldigen v excuse
entwerten v stamp (ticket)
entwickeln v develop (film)
epileptisch adj epileptic
erbrechen v vomit
erfahren adj experienced
erhalten receive
die Erkältung n cold
  (sickness)
erklären explain
erlauben allow
ernst serious
erreichen v reach
erschöpft exhausted
erstaunlich amazing
erste Klasse first class
erste adj first
erwärmen v warm (something)
essen eat
das Essen food
das Esszimmer dining room
die Etage floor [storey BE]
das E-Tioket e-ticket
etwas something;
  ~ mehr… some more…
der EU-Bürger EU resident
der Euro euro
die Exkursion excursion
der Experte n expert
der Express n express;
  ~bus express bus
extra extra; ~ groß extra large

die Fähre ferry
fahren v drive
die Fahrkarte ticket
der Fahrkartenschalter ticket
  office
das Fahrrad n bicycle
der Fahrradweg bike route
der Fahrstuhl elevator [lift BE]
die Fahrzeugregistrierung
  vehicle registration
die Familie family
die Farbe n color
das Fax n fax
faxen v fax
die Faxnummer fax number
der Fehler n mistake
fehlen be missing
der Urlaub vacation [holiday BE]
das Feinkostgeschäft
  delicatessen
das Fenster window
der Fernseher television
das Festpreismenü fixed
  price menu
die Festung fort
fettfrei fat free
das Feuer n fire
die Feuertür fire door
die Feuerwehr fire department
das Feuerzeug lighter
das Fieber fever
filetiert fileted (food)
der Film film (camera);
  ~ movie (cinema)

der **Finger** *n* finger
der **Fingernagel** fingernail
der **Fitnessraum** gym (workout)
die **Flasche** *n* bottle
der **Flaschenöffner** bottle opener
der **Fleischer** butcher
der **Florist** florist
der **Flug** flight
die **Fluggesellschaft** airline
der **Flughafen** airport
das **Flugzeug** airplane
der **Fluss** river
der **Fön** hair dryer
das **Förderband** conveyor belt
das **Formular** *n* form
fortgeschritten intermediate
das **Foto** photo
die **Fotografie** photography
fotografieren take a photo
die **Fotokopie** photocopy
die **Frage** *n* question
der **Franzbranntwein** rubbing alcohol [surgical spirit BE]
die **Frau** woman
freiberufliche Arbeit freelance work
frei *adj* free
das **Fremdenverkehrsbüro** tourist information office
die **Freude** pleasure
der **Freund** boyfriend; friend
die **Freundin** girlfriend; friend
frisch fresh
die **Frischhaltefolie** plastic wrap
der **Friseur** barber, hairstylist

der **Friseursalon** hair salon
die **Frisur** hairstyle
früh early
das **Frühstück** breakfast
der **Führer** guide
die **Führerscheinnummer** driver's license number
das **Fundbüro** lost-and-found
für for
der **Fuß** foot; **~ball** soccer
das **Fußballspiel** soccer match [football game BE]
der **Fußgänger** *n* pedestrian
das **Fußgelenk** *n* ankle
füttern *v* feed

G

die **Gabel** fork
der **Gang** aisle
die **Garage** garage
das **Gate** gate (airport)
das **Gebäude** building
geben *v* give
die **Gebühr** fee
der **Geburtstag** birthday
gefährlich dangerous
der **Gefrierschrank** freezer
das **Gegenteil** *n* opposite
gehen *v* go (somewhere)
gekocht stewed
das **Gel** gel (hair)
gelb *adj* yellow
das **Gelbgold** yellow gold
das **Geld** money
die **Geldbörse** wallet

der Geldschein *n* bill [note BE]
(money)
das Gelenk joint (body part)
das Generikum generic drug
[unbranded medication BE]
genießen *v* enjoy
das Gepäck baggage
[luggage BE]
die Gepäckausgabe baggage
claim
der Gepäckschein baggage
[luggage BE] ticket
das Gepäckschließfach
baggage [luggage BE] locker
der Gepäckwagen baggage
[luggage BE] cart
geradeaus straight
gern geschehen you're welcome
das Geschäft business; ~ store
~**sverzeichnis** store directory;
~**szentrum** business center
das Geschenk gift
der Geschenkwarenladen gift
shop
das Geschirr dishes (kitchen)
der Geschirrspüler dishwasher
das Geschirrspülmittel
dishwashing liquid
geschlossen closed
**die Geschwindigkeitsüber-
schreitung** speeding
das Gesicht *n* face
gestern yesterday
gestohlen stolen
die Gesundheit health
das Getränk *n* drink

die Getränkekarte drink menu
getrennt lebend separated
(person)
das Gewitter thunderstorm
gewürfelt diced (food)
das Gift *n* poison
der Gipfel peak (of a mountain)
das Girokonto checking
[current BE] account
das Glas glass
gleich same
glücklich happy
die Glühbirne lightbulb
golden golden
der Golfplatz golf course
das Golfturnier golf tournament
das Grad degree (temperature)
das Gramm gram
grau *adj* gray
der Grill *n* barbecue
groß big; ~ large
großartig magnificent
das Großbritannien United
Kingdom (U.K.)
die Größe *n* size
die Großeltern grandparents
größer bigger; ~ larger
grün *adj* green
die Gruppe *n* group
gültig valid
der Gürtel belt
gut *adj* good; *adv* well;
~**en Abend** good evening;
~**en Morgen** good morning;
~**en Tag** good day
der Gynäkologe gynecologist

das Haar hair
die Haarbürste hairbrush
der Harfestiger mousse (hair)
der Haarschnitt haircut
das Haarspray hairspray
haben *v* have
halal halal
halb half; ~gar underdone;
  die ~e Stunde half hour;
  das ~e Kilo half-kilo
die Halbschuhe loafers
halbtags part-time
das Hallenbad indoor pool
Hallo hello
der Hals throat
die Halsschmerzen sore
  throat
die Haltestelle *n* stop
der Hammer *n* hammer
die Hand *n* hand
das Handgelenk wrist
das Handgepäck hand
  luggage
die Handtasche purse
  [handbag BE]
das Handtuch towel
Handwäsche hand wash
das Handy cell [mobile BE]
  phone
hässlich ugly
die Hauptattraktion main
  attraction
das Hauptgericht main
  course

das Haus *n* house
das Haushaltsgerät utensil
die Haushaltswaren
  household goods
die Haut *n* skin
heiraten *v* marry
heiß hot (temperature);
  ~e Quelle hot spring;
  ~es Wasser hot water
heizen *v* heat
die Heizung heating
der Hektar hectare
helfen *v* help
der Helm helmet
das Hemd shirt
der Herd stove
das Herz heart
die Herzkrankheit heart
  condition
der Heuschnupfen hay fever
heute today; ~ Abend tonight
hier here
die Hilfe *n* help
die Hin- und Rückfahrt
  round-trip
Hinfahrt- one-way (ticket)
hinter behind (direction)
hoch high
das Hockey hockey
die Höhle *n* cave
hörgeschädigt hearing
  impaired
die Hose pants [trousers BE]
das Hotel hotel
hungrig hungry
husten *v* cough

der Husten *n* cough
der Hut hat

das Ibuprofen ibuprofen
die Identifikation identification
die Impfung vaccination
in in
infiziert infected
die Information information; ~ information desk
inländisch domestic
der Inlandsflug domestic flight
das Insekt bug
der Insektenschutz insect repellent
der Insektenstich insect bite
die Instant Message instant message
das Insulin insulin
interessant interesting
international international; **der ~e Studentenausweis** international student card; **der ~e Flug** international flight
das Internet internet; ~café internet cafe
der Internet-service internet service
irisch *adj* Irish
Irland Ireland
italienisch *adj* Italian

ja yes
die Jacke jacket
das Jahr year
japanisch Japanese
der Jazz jazz; ~club jazz club
die Jeans jeans
der Jeansstoff denim
der Jet-ski jet ski
jetzt now
die Jugendherberge hostel; ~ youth hostel
jung *adj* young
der Junge boy
der Juwelier jeweler

das Kabarett cabaret
das Kaffeehaus coffee house
die Kalorie calorie
kalt *adj* cold (temperature); ~ cool (temperature)
die Kamera camera
die Kameratasche camera case
der Kamm *n* comb
das Kanada Canada
kanadisch *adj* Canadian
die Karaffe carafe
die Karte *n* card; ~ map
der Kassierer cashier
der Kater hangover (alcohol)
die Kathedrale cathedral
kaufen *v* buy

das **Kaufhaus** department store

der **Kaugummi** chewing gum

der **Kellner** waiter

die **Kellnerin** waitress

die **Kette** necklace

der **Kiefer** jaw

das **Kilo** kilo; ~gramm kilogram

der **Kilometer** kilometer

das **Kind** child

der **Kinderarzt** pediatrician

das **Kinderbecken** kiddie pool

das **Kinderbett** cot

die **Kinderkarte** children's menu

die **Kinderportion** children's portion

der **Kindersitz** highchair

der **Kinderstuhl** child's seat; der **Kinderwagen** stroller

das **Kino** movie theater

die **Kirche** church

das **Kissen** pillow

die **Klarsichtfolie** plastic wrap [cling film BE]

die **Klasse** class

die **klassische Musik** classical music

das **Kleid** n dress (clothing)

die **Kleiderordnung** dress code

klein small

der **Kleintransporter** van

die **Klimaanlage** air conditioning

die **Klippe** cliff

das **Kloster** monastery

das **Knie** n knee

der **Knochen** n bone

kochen v boil; ~ cook

das **Kölnischwasser** cologne

der **Koffer** suitcase

der **Kollege** colleague

kommen v come

die **Konditorei** pastry shop

das **Kondom** condom

die **Konferenz** conference

das **Konferenzzimmer** meeting room

der **Kongressaal** convention hall

die **Konserve** canned good

das **Konsulat** consulate

kontaktieren v contact

die **Kontaktlinse** contact lens

die **Kontaktlinsenlösung** contact lens solution

das **Konto** n account

das **Konzert** concert

die **Konzerthalle** concert hall

der **Kopf** n head (body part)

die **Kopfhörer** headphones

die **Kopfschmerzen** headache

der **Korkenzieher** corkscrew

koscher kosher

kosmetisch adj cosmetic; ~e **Gesichtsbehandlung** facial (treatment)

kosten *v* cost; ~ taste
krank ill; ~ sick
das Krankenhaus hospital
die Krankenschwester *n* nurse
der Krankenwagen ambulance
die Krawatte tie (clothing)
die Kreditkarte credit card
die Kreuzung intersection
das Kriegsdenkmal war memorial
das Kristall crystal (glass)
die Küche kitchen
die Küchenmaschine food processor
der Kühlschrank refrigerator
die Kunst art
das Kupfer copper
kurz short; ~**e Hose** shorts
kurzärmelig short-sleeved
kurzsichtig near- [short- BE] sighted
küssen *v* kiss

L

laktoseintolerant lactose intolerant
die Lampe *n* light (overhead)
die Landesvorwahl country code
landwirtschaftliches Erzeugnis produce
lang *adj* long; ~**ärmlig** long-sleeved;

langsam slow; ~**er** slower
langweilig boring
der Laufstall playpen
lauter louder
leben *v* live
das Lebensmittelgeschäft grocery store
die Leber liver (body part)
lecker delicious
das Leder leather
leicht easy
das Leinen linen
leise quiet
die Lektion lesson
letzte *adj* last
die Liebe *n* love
lieben *v* love (someone)
der Liegestuhl deck chair (ferry)
der Liftpass lift pass
die Linie line (train)
links left (direction)
die Linse lens
die Lippe lip
der Liter liter
Livemusik live music
locker loose (fit)
der Löffel *n* spoon
löschen *v* clear (on an ATM); ~ *v* delete (computer)
die Lotion lotion
die Luftpost *n* airmail
die Luftpumpe air pump
lufttrocknen *v* air dry
die Lunge lung

das **Mädchen** girl
das **Magazin** magazine
der **Magen** stomach
die **Magenverstimmung**
upset stomach
die **Mahlzeit** meal
der **Manager** manager
die **Maniküre** *n* manicure
der **Mann** man (male)
der **Mantel** *n* coat
der **Markt** market
maschinentrocknen tumble
dry
die **Massage** *n* massage
mechanisch *adj* mechanic
das **Medikament** medicine
die **Medikamente**
medication
medium *adj* medium (meat)
das **Meer** sea
mehr more
die **Mehrwertsteuer** sales tax
[VAT BE]
die **Menstruationskrämpfe**
menstrual cramps
die **Messe** mass (church
service)
messen *v* measure
(someone)
das **Messer** knife
der **Messbecher** measuring
cup
der **Messlöffel** measuring
spoon

das **Mietauto** rental [hire BE]
car
mieten *v* rent [hire BE]
die **Mikrowelle** *n* microwave
mild mild
die **Mini-Bar** mini-bar
die **Minute** minute
mit with; ~ **Bedienung**
full-service
die **Mitgliedskarte**
membership card
mitkommen *v* join
mitnehmen give somebody a
lift (ride)
Mittag noon [midday BE]
das **Mittagessen** *n* lunch
Mitternacht midnight
der **Mixer** blender
die **Mobilität** mobility
mögen *v* like
der **Monat** month
die **Monatsbinde** sanitary
napkin [pad BE]
der **Mopp** *n* mop
das **Moped** moped
morgen tomorrow
der **Morgen** morning
die **Moschee** mosque
der **Moslem** Muslim
das **Motorboot** motor boat
das **Motorrad** motorcycle
das **Mountainbike** mountain
bike
müde tired
der **Mund** mouth
die **Münze** coin

das **Münztelefon** pay phone
das **Museum** museum
die **Musik** music
das **Musikgeschäft** music store
der **Muskel** muscle
die **Mutter** mother

N

nach after
der **Nachmittag** afternoon
nachprüfen *v* check (on something)
die **Nachricht** message
nachschneiden trim (haircut)
nächste *adj* next
die **Nacht** night
der **Nachtclub** nightclub
der **Nacken** neck
die **Nagelfeile** nail file
das **Nagelstudio** nail salon
nahe *prep* near
die **Nähe** vicinity; in der Nähe nearby
der **Name** *n* name
die **Nase** nose
die **Nationalität** nationality
das **Naturreservat** nature preserve
die **Nebenstelle** extension (phone)
die **Nebenwirkung** side effect
nehmen *v* take

nein no
Nichtraucher- non-smoking (area)
nichts nothing
niedrig low
die **Niere** kidney (body part)
der **Norden** *n* north
normal regular
der **Notausgang** emergency exit
der **Notfall** emergency
die **Nummer** *n* number
nur only; ~ just

O

obere *adj* upper
der **Oberschenkel** thigh
offen *adj* open
öffentlich *adj* public
öffnen *v* open
die **Öffnungszeiten** business hours
ohne without
das **Ohr** ear
die **Ohrenschmerzen** earache
der **Ohrring** earring
OK okay
das **Öl** *n* oil
die **Oper** opera
das **Opernhaus** opera house
der **Optiker** optician
orange *adj* orange (color)
das **Orchester** orchestra
die **Ortsvorwahl** area code
der **Osten** *n* east

packen *v* pack
die Packung carton; ~ packet
das Paket package
der Palast palace
paniert breaded
die Panne breakdown (car)
die Pantoffeln slippers
das Papier *n* paper
das Papierhandtuch paper towel
das Paracetamol acetaminophen [paracetamol BE]
das Parfüm *n* perfume
der Park *n* park
parken *v* park
das Parkhaus parking garage
der Parkplatz parking lot [car park BE]
die Parkuhr parking meter
das Parlamentsgebäude parliament building
das Parterre ground floor
der Passagier passenger
die Passform fit (clothing)
die Passkontrolle passport control
das Passwort password
die Pediküre pedicure
das Penicillin penicillin
der Penis penis
die Pension bed and breakfast
die Periode period (menstrual)

die Perle pearl
der Pfad path
die Pferderennbahn horsetrack
das Pflaster bandage
das Pfund *n* pound (weight)
das Pfund pound (British sterling)
die Pille Pill (birth control)
die Piste *n* trail [piste BE]
der Pistenplan trail [piste BE] map
die Pizzeria pizzeria
der Plan *n* schedule [timetable BE]; ~ map
planen *v* plan
das Platin platinum
der Platte flat tire
der Platz field (sports); ~ seat; ~ am Gang aisle seat
die Plombe filling (tooth)
der Po buttocks
die Polizei police
der Polizeibericht police report
das Polizeirevier police station
der Pool *n* pool
die Popmusik pop music
die Portion *n* portion
die Post mail [post BE]; ~ post office
die Postkarte postcard
der Preis price; ~ pro Gedeck cover charge
preisgünstig inexpensive

pro per; **~ Nacht** per night;
  ~ Stunde per hour; **~ Tag** per
  day; **~ Woche** per week
das Problem problem
Prost! Cheers!
die Prothese denture
die Puppe doll
der Pyjama pajamas

Q

die Qualität n quality
die Quittung receipt

R

das R-Gespräch collect call
  [reverse charge call BE]
ein R-Gespräch führen v call
  collect [to reverse the charges
  BE]
der Rabatt discount
das Radfahren cycling
der Rap rap (music)
die Rasiercreme shaving
  cream
die Rasierklinge razor blade
der Rastplatz picnic area
das Rathaus town hall
der Rathausplatz town
  square
rauchen v smoke
Raucher- smoking (area)
die Rechnung bill [invoice BE]
  (of sale)
rechts right (direction)

das Recycling recycling
das Reformhaus health food
  store
der Regen n rain
die Regenjacke raincoat
der Regenschirm umbrella
der Regenwald rainforest
die Region region
regnerisch rainy
der Reifen tire [tyre BE]
reinigen v clean;
  chemisch ~ dry clean
die Reinigung dry cleaner's
die Reinigungsmittel cleaning
  supplies
die Reise trip; **~** journey
das Reisebüro travel agency
der Reiseführer guide book
die Reisekrankheit motion
  sickness
der Reisepass passport
der Reisescheck traveler's
  check [cheque BE]
die Rennbahn racetrack
der Rentner senior citizen
reparieren v fix; **~** repair
reservieren v reserve
die Reservierung reservation
der Reservierungsschalter
  reservation desk
das Restaurant restaurant
der Rettungsschwimmer
  lifeguard
das Rezept prescription
die Rezeption reception
die Richtung direction

der Ring *n* ring
die Rippe rib (body part)
der Rock skirt
der Rollstuhl wheelchair
die Rollstuhlrampe
 wheelchair ramp
die Rolltreppe escalator
romantisch romantic
rosa *adj* pink
rot *adj* red
die Route route
der Rücken *n* back (body part)
die Rückenschmerzen
 backache
der Rucksack backpack
das Ruderboot rowboat
das Rugby rugby
die Ruine ruin

S

der Safe *n* safe (for valuables)
die Sandalen sandals
sauber *adj* clean
die Sauerstoffbehandlung
 oxygen treatment
die Saugglocke plunger
die Sauna sauna
der Scanner scanner
die Schachtel *n* pack; ~
 Zigaretten pack of cigarettes
der Schal scarf
scharf hot (spicy); ~ sharp
das Schaufenster window
 case
der Scheck *n* check
 [cheque BE] (payment)

die Schere scissors
schicken send;
 per Post ~ mail
das Schlachtfeld battleground
schlafen *v* sleep
die Schläfrigkeit drowsiness
der Schlafsack sleeping bag
die Schlafstörung insomnia
der Schlafwagen sleeper
 [sleeping BE] car
der Schläger racket (sports)
schlecht nauseous; ~ bad
der Schlepplift drag lift
schließen *v* close (a shop)
das Schließfach locker
das Schloss castle; ~ lock
die Schlucht ravine
der Schlüssel key; ~ring
 key ring
die Schlüsselkarte key card
der Schmerz pain;
Schmerzen haben be in pain
der Schmuck jewelry
schmutzig dirty
der Schneeschuh snowshoe
schneiden *v* cut
schnell fast
der Schnellzug express train
der Schnitt *n* cut (injury)
der Schnuller pacifier
 [soother BE]
schön nice; ~ beautiful
schrecklich terrible
schreiben write
der Schrein shrine

der Schuh shoe
das Schuhgeschäft shoe store
die Schule school
die Schulter shoulder
die Schüssel bowl
schwanger pregnant
schwarz *adj* black
die Schwellung swelling
die Schwester sister
schwierig difficult
das Schwimmbad swimming pool
schwimmen *v* swim
die Schwimmweste life jacket
schwindelig dizzy
schwul *adj* gay
die Schwulenbar gay bar
der Schwulenclub gay club
der See lake
sehbehindert visually impaired
sehen *v* look; ~ see
die Sehenswürdigkeit attraction
die Seide silk
die Seife *n* soap
die Seilbahn cable car
sein *v* be
die Selbstbedienung self-service
selten rare
seltsam strange
das Seminar seminar

senden *v* send
die Serviette napkin
der Sessellift chair lift
sexuell übertragbare Krankheit sexually transmitted disease (STD)
das Shampoo *n* shampoo
sich scheiden lassen *v* divorce
sicher *adj* safe (protected)
die Sicherheit security
das Sieb colander
das Sightseeing sightseeing
das Silber *n* silver
sitzen *v* sit
der Ski *n* ski
Ski fahren *v* ski
der Skilift ski lift
der Slip briefs (clothing)
die SMS SMS; eine SMS schicken *v* text (message)
das Snowboard *n* snowboard
die Socke sock
die Sonne *n* sun
der Sonnenbrand sunburn
die Sonnenbrille sunglasses
die Sonnencreme sunscreen
der Sonnenstich sunstroke
sonnig sunny
das Souvenir souvenir; ~geschäft souvenir store
das Sparkonto savings (account)
spät late (time)
der Spatel spatula

später later
spazieren gehen *v* walk
der Spaziergang *n* walk
die Speicherkarte memory card
speichern *v* save (computer)
die Speisekarte menu
der Spezialist specialist (doctor)
das Spiel game; ~ match
spielen *v* play
die Spielhalle arcade
der Spielplatz playground
das Spielzeug toy
der Spielzeugladen toy store
das Spirituosengeschäft liquor store [off-licence BE]
die Spitze lace (fabric)
der Sport sports
die Sportmassage sports massage
das Sportgeschäft sporting goods store
sprechen *v* speak
der Springbrunnen fountain
die Spülung conditioner (hair)
die Stäbchen chopsticks
das Stadion stadium
die Stadt city; ~ town
der Stadtplan town map
die Stadtrundfahrt sightseeing tour
das Stadtzentrum downtown area
die Stange carton (of cigarettes)

die Statue statue
der Staubsauger vacuum cleaner
das Steakhouse steakhouse
die Steckdose electric outlet
stehlen *v* steal
steil steep
das Sterlingsilber sterling silver
der Stich *n* sting
die Stiefel boots
der Stift pen
stillen breastfeed
die Stöcke poles (skiing)
stornieren *v* cancel
die Strafe *n* fine (fee for breaking law)
die Strähnchen highlights (hair)
der Strand beach
die Straßenkarte road map
der Strom electricity
die Strumpfhose pantyhose [tights BE]
das Stück *n* piece; ~ play (theater); ~ slice
der Student student
studieren *v* study
der Stuhl chair
der Stuhlgang stool (bowel movement)
die Stunde hour
der Süden *n* south
das Super super (fuel)
der Supermarkt supermarket
das Surfboard surfboard

das Surfbrett windsurfer (board)
süß cute; ~ sweet (taste)
die Süßigkeit candy [sweet BE]
das Sweatshirt sweatshirt
die Synagoge synagogue
synchronisiert dubbed

T

der Tabakhändler tobacconist
die Tablette tablet (medicine)
der Tag day
Tages- one-day (ticket)
das Tal valley
der Tampon tampon
tanken *v* fill (car)
die Tankstelle gas [petrol BE] station
der Tanzclub dance club
tanzen *v* dance
die Tasche bag; ~ pocket
die Tasse *n* cup
taub *adj* deaf
die Tauchausrüstung diving equipment
tauchen *v* dive
das Taxi taxi
das Team team
der Teelöffel teaspoon
der Teich pond
das Teil part (for car)
das Telefon *n* phone
das schnurlose Telefon wireless phone

der Telefonanruf phone call
die Telefonkarte phone card
die Telefonnummer phone number
der Teller plate
der Tempel temple (religious)
das Tennis tennis
der Termin appointment
der Terminal terminal (airport)
teuer expensive
der Text *n* text
das Theater theater
tief deep
die Tiefkühlkost frozen food
das Tier animal
der Tisch table
die Toilette restroom [toilet BE]
das Toilettenpapier toilet paper
der Topf *n* pot
die Töpferwaren pottery (pots)
die Tour *n* tour
der Tourist tourist
traditionell traditional
traurig sad
treffen meet
das Treffen meeting
trennen disconnect (computer)
die Treppe stairs
trinken *v* drink
das Trinkwasser drinking water
der Tropfen *n* drop (medicine)
das T-Shirt T-shirt

die Tür door
der Turm tower
die Turnschuhe sneaker

U

die U-Bahn subway
[underground BE]
die U-Bahn-Haltestelle
subway [underground BE]
station
über *prep* over;
~ Nacht overnight;
~fallen *v* mug
die Übergröße plus size
überhitzen overheat (car)
übersetzen translate
überweisen *v* transfer
(money)
um (die Ecke) around (the
corner)
umändern alter
umarmen *v* hug
die Umkleidekabine fitting
room
der Umschlag envelope
umsteigen *v* change (buses);
~ *v* transfer (change trains/
flights)
umtauschen *v* exchange
(money)
umwerfend stunning
unbeaufsichtigt
unattended
der Unfall accident
die Universität university

die Unterhaltung
entertainment (amusement)
die Unterhose underwear
[underpants BE]
die Unterkunft
accommodation
die Unterlegplane
groundcloth
unterschreiben *v* sign
der Untertitel *n* subtitle
die Unterwäsche underwear
der Urin urine
der Urlaub vacation [BE
holiday]

V

die Vagina vagina
vaginal vaginal; die ~e
Entzündung vaginal
infection
der Vater father
der V-Ausschnitt V-neck
der Veganer *n* vegan
der Vegetarier *n* vegetarian
der Ventilator fan
(appliance)
verbieten *v* prohibit
verbinden *v* connect
(internet)
die Verbindung connection
die Vereinigten
Staaten United States
(U.S.)
verfügbar available

vergewaltigen *v* rape
die Vergewaltigung *n* rape
der Vergnügungspark
amusement park
verheiratet married
verkaufen *v* sell
verlangen *v* charge (cost)
verlieren *v* lose (something)
verlobt engaged
verloren lost
verschlucken *v* swallow
verschneit snowy
verschreiben *v* prescribe
(medication)
versenden *v* ship
die Versicherung insurance
die Versicherungsgesellschaft
insurance company
die Versicherungskarte
insurance card
die Verstauchung *n* sprain
verstehen understand
die Verstopfung
constipation
verwitwet widowed
verzögern *v* delay
viel much; ~ a lot;
~en Dank thank you;
wie ~ how much
violett *adj* purple
die Visitenkarte business
card
das Visum visa
das Vitamin vitamin
die Vitrine display case
der Vogel bird

die Volksmusik folk music
das Volleyballspiel volleyball
game
Vollzeit- full-time
vor before; **Viertel ~ vier** a
quarter to four
die Vorfahrt right of way
die Vorhersage *n* forecast
die Vorspeise appetizer
[starter BE]
vorstellen *v* introduce
(person)
vorübergehend temporary

W

wählen *v* dial
während during
die Währung currency
der Währungsumtausch
currency exchange
der Wald forest
die Wanderroute walking
route
die Wanderschuhe hiking
boots
die Wanduhr wall clock
wann when (time)
die Ware *n* good; ~ product
die Waren goods
warm *adj* warm
(temperature)
warten wait
der Warteraum waiting room
die Wartezeit *n* waiting
period

was what
das Waschbecken *n* sink
die Wäscherei laundry
(facility)
der Wäscheservice laundry
service
die Waschmaschine washing
machine
waschmaschinenfest machine
washable
das Waschmittel detergent
der Waschsalon laundromat
[launderette BE]
der Wasserfall waterfall
die Wasserski water skis
das Wechselgeld *n* change
(money)
der Wechselkurs exchange
rate
wechseln *v* change
die Wechselstube currency
exchange office
wecken *v* wake
der Weckruf wake-up call
weich soft
das Weingut vineyard
die Weinkarte wine list
weiß *adj* white
das Weißgold white gold
weit *adv* far (distance);
~ *adj* loose (fit)
weitsichtig far [long BE]-
sighted
das Wellness-Center spa
wenig *adj* little (not much)

weniger less
wer who
der Wert value
wertvoll valuable
der Westen *n* west
das Wetter weather
wickeln *v* change (baby)
wie how; ~ **viel** how much
wiederholen repeat
willkommen *adj* welcome
die Windel diaper [nappy BE]
die Wirbelsäule spine
(body part)
wireless wireless
wo where
die Woche week
das Wochenende weekend
wöchentlich weekly
der Wohnwagen mobile
home
die Wolle wool
wunder schön beautiful
die Wüste *n* desert

Z

der Zahn tooth
der Zahnarzt dentist
die Zahnpaste toothpaste
der Zeh *n* toe
der Zehennagel toenail
das Zeichen symbol
(keyboard)
zeigen *v* show (somebody
something)
die Zeit time

der Zeitraum period (of time)
die Zeitung newspaper
der Zeitungskiosk newsstand
das Zelt tent
der Zelthering tent peg
die Zeltstange tent pole
der Zentimeter centimeter
zerbrochen broken (smashed)
das Zertifikat certificate
ziehen *v* extract (tooth);
  ~ *v* pull (door sign)
die Zigarette cigarette
die Zigarre cigar
das Zimmer room

der Zimmerschlüssel room
  key
der Zimmerservice room
  service
das Zinn pewter
der Zoll customs; ~ duty (tax)
zollfrei duty-free
der Zoo zoo
zu *adv* too; ~ *prep* to
der Zug train
die Zunge tongue
zurückgeben *v* return
  (something)
der Zutritt *n* access